A Narrative of a Nine Months' Residence in New Zealand

Augustus Earle

A New Zealand War Speech. (From a sketch by A. Earle.

A NARRATIVE OF A NINE MONTHS' RESIDENCE IN NEW ZEALAND

IN 1827

BY

AUGUSTUS EARLE

DRAUGHTSMAN TO HIS MAJESTY'S SURVEYING SHIP

"THE BEAGLE."

Whitecombe & Tombs Limited

Christchurch, Wellington, and Dunedin, N.Z.;

Melbourne and London

1909

CONTENTS

MAORI WOMEN'S CAMP

CHAPTER XX
LOADING SPARS, HOKIANGA

CHAPTER XXI
DEATH OF A CHIEF
TRADING WITH MAORIS

CHAPTER XXII
BRUTAL MURDER OF A WIFE

CHAPTER XXIII
ANOTHER JOURNEY
INTERIOR OF THE COUNTRY

CHAPTER XXIV
A WAR PARTY

CHAPTER XXV
HOSTILE DISPLAY
THE LAW OF MURU

CHAPTER XXVI
A SEDUCTION AND ITS CONSEQUENCES

CHAPTER XXVII
LAW OF RETALIATION

CHAPTER XXVIII
A WAR EXPEDITION
CANNIBALISM

CHAPTER XXIX
MAORI SLAVERY

CHAPTER XXX
PIRACY BY CONVICTS

LIST OF ILLUSTRATIONS.

INTRODUCTION

The author of this account of New Zealand in the year 1827 was an artist by profession. "A love of roving and adventure," he states, tempted him, at an early age, to sea. In 1815 he procured a passage on board a storeship bound for Sicily and Malta, where he had a brother stationed who was a captain in the navy. He visited many parts of the Mediterranean, accompanying Lord Exmouth's fleet in his brother's gunboat on his Lordship's first expedition against the Barbary States. He afterwards visited the ruins of Carthage and the remains of the ancient city of Ptolomea, or Lepida, situated in ancient Libya. Returning to Malta, he passed through Sicily, and ascended Mount Etna. In 1818 he left England for the United States, and spent nearly two years in rambling through that country. Thence he proceeded to Brazil and Chile, returning to Rio de Janeiro, where he practised his art until the commencement of 1824. Having received letters of introduction to Lord Amherst, who had left England to undertake the government of India, Mr. Earle left Rio for the Cape of Good Hope, intending to take his passage thence to Calcutta. On the voyage to the Cape the vessel by which he was a passenger touched at Tristan d'Acunha, and was driven off that island in a gale while Mr. Earle was ashore, leaving him stranded in that desolate land, where he remained for six months, when he was rescued by a passing ship, the "Admiral Cockburn," bound for Van Diemen's Land, whence he visited New South Wales and New Zealand, returning again to Sydney. In pursuance of his original resolution to visit India, he left Sydney in "The Rainbow," touching at the Caroline Islands, Manilla, and Singapore. After spending some time in Madras, where he executed many original drawings, which were afterwards copied and exhibited in a panorama, he set out for England by a French vessel, which was compelled by stress of weather to put into Mauritius, where she was condemned. Mr. Earle ultimately reached England in a vessel named the "Resource," but, being still animated by the desire for travel, he accepted the situation of draughtsman on His Majesty's ship "Beagle," commanded by Captain Fitzroy, which in the year 1831 left on a voyage of discovery that has been made famous by the observations of Charles Darwin, who accompanied the expedition in the capacity of naturalist.

The notes which furnished the materials for this book were made by Mr. Earle during his first visit to New Zealand, in 1827. They are valuable as setting forth the impressions formed by an educated man, who came into the primitive community then existing at Hokianga and the Bay of Islands, without being personally connected either with the trading community, the missionaries, or the whalers. It should not be inferred from the reflections Mr. Earle casts upon the missionaries that he was himself an irreligious man, because the journal of his residence on Tristan d'Acunha shows that, while living there, he read the whole service of the Church of England to that little community every Sunday, and his diary in many places exhibits a reverence for Divine things. It may, however, be said in extenuation of the lack of hospitality on the part of the missionaries of which he complains, that many of the early residents and European visitors to New Zealand were of an undesirable class, and that they exercised a demoralising influence upon the Maoris. It was not easy for the missionaries to consort, upon terms of intimacy, with their fellow-countrymen whose relations with the Natives were such as they must strongly condemn. Earle's narrative is interesting because it conveys a realistic description of the Maoris before their national customs and habits had undergone any material change through association with white settlers. In dealing with Maori names, Mr. Earle, having at that period no standard of orthography to guide him, followed the example of Captain Cook in spelling words phonetically. Except in the case of certain well-known places the original spelling has been retained in the present edition of his book.

CHAPTER I

VOYAGE FROM SYDNEY

Having made up my mind to visit the island of New Zealand, and having persuaded my friend Mr. Shand to accompany me, we made an arrangement for the passage with Captain Kent, of the brig Governor Macquarie, and, bidding adieu to our friends at Sydney, in a few hours (on October 20th, 1827) we were wafted into the great Pacific Ocean.

There were several other passengers on board, who were proceeding to New Zealand to form a Wesleyan missionary establishment at Hokianga. Amongst these were a Mr. and Mrs. Hobbs, who were most enthusiastic in the cause. They had formerly belonged to the same mission at Whangaroa, when a war which took place amongst the natives totally destroyed their establishment; and, after enduring great varieties of suffering, they escaped, but lost everything they possessed, except the clothes they had on. We had a very fine wind for nine days, and on the 29th we saw a gannet, a sure sign we were within a hundred miles of land, for these birds are never seen at a greater distance from it. True to our anticipations, towards the afternoon the water became discoloured, and at midnight we saw the land.

This interesting island, of which we now got sight, was first discovered by that eminent and enterprising Dutch navigator, Tasman, subsequently to the discovery of Van Diemen's Land. His voyage from Batavia in 1642, undertaken by order of the then Governor-General of Dutch India, Anthony Van Diemen, was one of the most important and successful ever undertaken, for it was during this voyage that New Holland was discovered, of which Van Diemen's Land was then supposed to form a part, the extensive island of New Zealand being supposed to form another portion.[1]

The slight intercourse of the discoverers with the natives had so calamitous a termination, and the exaggerated accounts it was then a kind of fashion to give of savages, stigmatised the New Zealanders with such a character for treachery and cruelty, that their island was not visited again for upwards of a century, when the immortal Cook drew aside the veil of error and obscurity from this unexplored land, and rescued the character of its inhabitants from the ignominy which its original discoverers, the Dutch, had thrown upon them. This immense tract of land was imagined by Tasman to form but one island, and he most unaptly gave it the name of New Zealand, from its great resemblance (as was stated) to his own country.[2]

In 1770 Cook discovered a strait of easy access and safe navigation, cutting the island nearly in half, thus making two islands of what had before been imagined but one. This strait bears his name, and is often traversed by vessels from New South Wales returning home by way of Cape Horn.

In 1827 His Majesty's ship Warsprite passed through this strait in company with the Volage, twenty-eight guns, being the first English line of battleship which had ever made the attempt. A few years since, Captain Stewart, commanding a colonial vessel out of Port Jackson, discovered another strait, which cut off the extreme southern point, making it a separate island that bears his name, and now almost every year our sealers and whalers are making additional and useful discoveries along its coasts.

These islands lie between lat. 34° and 48°S. and long. 166° and 180°E. The opening of the land to which we were now opposite, and which was our destined port, the accurate eye of Cook had observed, but did not attempt the entrance; and it is only about ten years since, when the two store ships, the Dromedary and Coromandel, loaded with spars on the coast, that a small vessel attending on those ships first crossed the bar; but although they took soundings and laid down buoys, the commanders of the large vessels were afraid of attempting the entrance, which proved their good sense, for their great draught of water would have rendered the undertaking more hazardous than the risk was worth. Yet during my residence in this country two large vessels crossed the bar, and recrossed it heavily laden, without the slightest accident—one the Harmony, of London, 400 tons burden; the other the Elizabeth, of Sydney, of nearly equal tonnage—but in proof that it is not always safe, a few months after this, two schooners of extremely light draught were lost, though they were both commanded by men who perfectly well knew the channels through the bar. It was a singular circumstance that both vessels had been built in New Zealand; one, the Herald, a small and beautiful craft, built by and belonging to the Church missionaries, the crew of which escaped, but the disastrous circumstances attending the wreck of the other, called the Enterprise, I shall relate in their proper place.

The morning of the 30th was foggy and unfavourable, but it suddenly cleared up, and exhibited the entrance of Hokianga right before us, and a light breeze came to our aid to carry us in. The entrance to this river is very remarkable, and can never be mistaken by mariners. On the north side, for many miles, are hills of sand, white, bleak, and barren, ending abruptly at the entrance of the river, which is about a quarter of a mile across. Where the south head rises abrupt, craggy, and black, the land all round is covered with verdure; thus, at the first glimpse of these heads from the sea, one is white, the other black.

The only difficulty attending the entrance (and, indeed, the only thing which prevents Hokianga from being one of the finest harbours in the world) is the bar. This lies two miles from the mouth of the river, its head enveloped in breakers and foam, bidding defiance and threatening destruction to all large ships which may attempt the passage. However, we fortunately slipped over its sandy sides, undamaged, in three-fathom water.

After crossing the bar, no other obstacle lay in our way, and, floating gradually into a beautiful river, we soon lost sight of the sea, and were sailing up a spacious sheet of water, which became considerably wider after entering it; while majestic hills rose on each side, covered with verdure to their very summits. Looking up the river, we beheld various headlands stretching into the water, and gradually contracting in width, till they became fainter and fainter in the distance, and all was lost in the azure of the horizon. The excitement occasioned by contemplating these beautiful scenes was soon interrupted by the hurried approach of canoes, and the extraordinary noises made by the natives who were in them.

FOOTNOTES:

[1]

The Dutch and Spanish had discovered N.E. Australia as early as 1606, and the Dutch had on several occasions visited the N.W. and South coasts of the Continent before the date of Tasman's voyage.
[2]

The name given by Tasman was Staten Landt. The name New Zealand was bestowed in 1643 by the States-General of the United Provinces.

CHAPTER II

RECEPTION BY THE NATIVES

As the arrival of a ship is always a profitable occurrence, great exertions are made to be the first on board. There were several canoes pulling towards us, and from them a number of muskets were fired, a compliment we returned with our swivels; one of the canoes soon came alongside, and an old chief came on board, who rubbed noses with Captain Kent, whom he recognised as an old acquaintance; he then went round and shook hands with all the strangers, after which he squatted himself down upon the deck, seeming very much to enjoy the triumph of being the first on board. But others very soon coming up with us, our decks were crowded with them, some boarding us at the gangway, others climbing up the chains and bows, and finding entrances where they could. All were in perfect good humour, and pleasure beamed in all their countenances.

I had heard a great deal respecting the splendid race of men I was going to visit, and the few specimens I had occasionally met with at Sydney so much pleased me, that I was extremely anxious to see a number of them together, to judge whether (as a nation) they were finer in their proportions than the English, or whether it was mere accident that brought some of their tallest and finest proportioned men before me.

I examined these savages, as they crowded round our decks, with the critical eye of an artist; they were generally taller and larger men than ourselves; those of middle height were broad-chested and muscular, and their limbs as sinewy as though they had been occupied all their lives in laborious employments. Their colour is lighter than that of the American Indian, their features small and regular, their hair is in a profusion of beautiful curls, whereas that of the Indian is straight and lank. The disposition of the New Zealander appears to be full of fun and gaiety, while the Indian is dull, shy, and suspicious.

I have known Indians in America from the north to the south—the miserable, idiotic Botecooda of Brazil, the fierce warrior of Canada, and the gentle and civilised Peruvian, yet in their features and complexions they are all much alike. I observed their statures altered with their different latitudes; the Chilians and the Canadians being nearly the same, in figure tall, thin, and active, their climate being nearly the same, although at the two extremes of America; while those living between the equinoxes are short, fat, and lazy. I am persuaded that these South Sea Islanders, though so nearly of the same complexion, still are not of the same race, laziness being the characteristic of the American Indian from north to south, while the New Zealanders are laborious in the extreme, as their astonishing and minute carvings prove. The moment the Indian tasted intoxicating spirits his valour left him, he became an idiot and a tool in the hands of the white man. Here they have the utmost aversion to every kind of "wine or strong drink," and very often severely take us to task for indulging in such an extraordinary and debasing propensity, or, as they call it, "of making ourselves mad;" but both nations are equally fond of tobacco.

The first thing which struck me forcibly was, that each of these savages was armed with a good musket, and most of them had also a cartouch box buckled round their waists, filled with ball cartridges, and those who had fired their pieces from the canoes carefully cleaned the pans, covered the locks over with a piece of dry rag, and put them in a secure place in their canoes. Every person who has read Captain Cook's account of the natives of New Zealand would be astonished at the change which has taken place since his time, when the firing of a single musket would have terrified a whole village.

As we sailed up the river very slowly, the throng of savages increased to such a degree that we could scarcely move, and, to add to our confusion, they gave us "a dance of welcome," standing on one spot, and stamping so furiously that I really feared they would have stove in the decks, which our lady passengers were obliged to leave, as when the dance began each man proceeded to strip himself naked, a custom indispensable among themselves.

We came to an anchor off a native village called Pakanae, where two chiefs of consequence came on board, who soon cleared our decks of a considerable number. We paid great attention to these chiefs, admitting them into the cabin, etc., and it had the effect of lessening the noise, and bringing about some kind of order amongst those who still continued on deck. The names of these chiefs were Moetara and Akaeigh, and they were the heads of the village opposite to which we had anchored. They were well known to our captain, who spoke their language. They were accustomed to the society of Europeans, also to transact business with them; and as they were flax, timber, and hog merchants, they and the captain talked over the state of the markets during the evening. They were clothed in mats, called Kaka-hoos. The ladies joined our party at supper, and we spent a very cheerful time with our savage visitors, who both behaved in as polite and respectful a manner as the best educated gentlemen could have done; their pleasing manners so ingratiated them into the good opinion of the ladies, that they all declared "they would be really very handsome men if their faces were not tattooed."

The next day we received a visit from Mr. and Mrs. Butler, English people, who had taken up their residence here for the purpose of trading, and we returned with them on shore, taking our female passengers with us, and leaving them in charge of Mrs. Butler. I determined to stroll through the village, which is, in fact, a collection of rude huts, huddled together without system or regularity. Dock leaves and weeds of every description were growing luxuriantly all round them, and in many places actually overtopping the houses, few being more than four feet high, with a doorway about two feet. Scarcely any of them were inhabited, as at this season of the year the greater part of the population prefer living in the open air to remaining in their small, smoky ovens of houses.

I had not rambled far before I witnessed a scene which forcibly reminded me of the savage country in which I then was, and the great alteration of character and customs a few days' sail will make. The sight to me so appalling was that of the remains of a human body which had been roasted, and a number of hogs and dogs were snarling and feasting upon it! I was more shocked than surprised, for I had been informed of the character of the New Zealanders long before my arrival amongst them; still, the coming suddenly and unexpectedly upon a sight like this completely sickened me of rambling, at least for that day, and I hastened back to Mr. Butler's, eager to inquire into the particulars of the horrid catastrophe.

That gentleman informed me that the night of the arrival of our ship, a chief had set one of his kookies (or slaves) to watch a piece of ground planted with the kumara, or sweet potato, in order to prevent the hogs committing depredations upon it. The poor lad, delighted with the appearance of our vessel, was more intent upon observing her come to an anchor than upon guarding his master's property, and suffered the hogs to ramble into the plantation, where they soon made dreadful havoc. In the midst of this trespass and neglect of orders his master arrived. The result was certain; he instantly killed the unfortunate boy with a blow on the head from his stone hatchet, then ordered a fire to be made, and the body to be dragged to it, where it was roasted and consumed.

It was now time to return on board, and we walked down to the beach for that purpose, but it was quite low water, and the boat was full two hundred feet off. She lay at the end of a long, slimy, muddy flat, and while we were debating how we should manage to get to her, the native chiefs took up the females in their arms, as though they were children, and, in spite of all their blushes and remonstrances, carried them to the boat and placed them safely in it, each seeming to enjoy the task. They then returned and gave us a passage, walking as easily with us upon their backs as if we had been no heavier than so many muskets. We took care not to shock the feelings of the females by letting them know the tragedy so lately acted in the village, or horrify them by telling them that one of their carriers was the murderer! It would have been difficult to have made them believe that such a noble-looking and good-natured fellow had so lately imbrued his hands in the blood of a fellow creature.

We had now been lying here two days, and the curiosity of the people did not diminish, nor were our visitors less numerous. Parties were hourly coming up and down the river to pay their respects to our captain, and the report of there being numerous passengers on board greatly increased their desire to hold intercourse with us. They all appeared anxious to make themselves useful, some chopping wood for our cook, others assisting the steward, in order to get what might be left on the plates, others brought small presents of fish; in fact, all availed themselves of any excuse to get on board; yet, notwithstanding the crowd, and the confusion attending their movements, there was scarcely any thieving amongst them. They have seen the detestation that theft is held in by Europeans, and the injury it does to trade, and have, in consequence, nearly left it off. None but the meanest slaves will now practise it, and they do so at the risk of their lives; for, if caught in the act, and the charge is proved against them, their heads are cut off!

CHAPTER III

A RAMBLE ASHORE

On November 3rd we visited Pakanae, a village lying round the base of a large conical hill, about three hundred feet high, with a fortification on the top, which gives it its name, pa signifying in their language a fortified place. Behind it lies a swamp, which is covered at high water, and which adds greatly to its security; for the unsettled and war-like spirit of the natives renders it absolutely necessary that they always should have a place of strength near at hand to retreat to, as they never know how suddenly their enemies may make an attack upon them. To the right of this swamp is a beautiful valley, in a very high state of cultivation. At the time I stood viewing it from the summit of the hill, I was charmed with the scene of industry and bustle it presented, all the inhabitants of the village having gone forth to plant their potatoes, kumaras, and Indian corn. In the rear, and forming a fine, bold background, is an immense chain of high and rugged hills, covered to their summits with thick forests, and forming, as it were, a natural barrier and protection to this smiling and fruitful valley, while from their wooded sides issue innumerable small streams of clear water, which, meeting at the base, form beautiful rivulets, and after meandering through the valley, and serving all the purposes of irrigation, they empty themselves into the Hokianga river.

Standing on the spot from which I have described the above prospect, I felt fully convinced of the frugality and industry of these savages. The regularity of their plantations, and the order with which they carry on their various works, differ greatly from most of their brethren in the South Seas, as here the chiefs and their families set the example of labour; and when that is the case, none can refuse to toil. Round the village of Pakanae, at one glance is to be seen above 200 acres of cultivated land, and that not slightly turned up, but well worked and cleared; and when the badness of their tools is considered, together with their limited knowledge of agriculture, their persevering industry I look upon as truly astonishing.

The New Zealanders have established here a wise custom, which prevents a great deal of waste and confusion, and generally preserves to the planter a good crop, in return for the trouble of sowing; namely, as soon as the ground is finished, and the seed sown, it is *tabooed*, that, is rendered sacred, by men appointed for that service, and it is death to trample over or disturb any part of this consecrated ground. The wisdom and utility of this regulation must be obvious to every one. But, however useful this taboo system is to the natives, it is a great inconvenience to a stranger who is rambling over the country, for if he does not use the greatest caution, and procure a guide, he may get himself into a serious dilemma before his rambles be over, which had nearly been the case with our party this day. We were ascending a hill, for the purpose of inspecting a New Zealand fortification on the summit, when a little boy joined our party, either out of curiosity, or in hopes of getting a fish-hook from us—a thing the natives are continually asking for; but as we had a man with us who spoke the language fluently, we did not much regard the boy's guidance, though to us it speedily became of great importance. We were taking a short cut, to make a quick ascent to the top of the hill, when the little fellow uttered a cry of horror. Our interpreter asked him what he meant, when he pointed his finger forward, and told him to look, for the ground was tabooed. We did as he desired us, but beheld nothing particular, till he showed us, in one of the trees, among the branches, a large bunch of something, but we could not make out what it was. This, he told us, was the body of a chief, then undergoing the process of decomposition, previous to interment, which process is witnessed by men appointed for that purpose, who alone are permitted to approach the spot. The ground all round is tabooed, so that, had it not been for the interference of our young guide, we should certainly have been placed in a most distressing situation; and it is a question if our ignorance of their customs would have been considered a sufficient excuse for our offence.

The top of this hill was level and square, and was capable of containing several hundred warriors. It was cut into slopes all round, and fortified by stockades in every direction, which rendered it impregnable. The natives assured me its strength had been often tried. The famous warrior Hongi had attacked it several times, but had always been defeated with great loss. After inspecting this fortification, which excited our admiration, we proceeded through the village at the bottom of the hill. Nearly the whole of the inhabitants were out working in the fields. We entered several of their habitations, and found all their property exposed and unguarded. Even their muskets and powder, which they prize above everything, were open to our inspection, so little idea of robbery have they amongst themselves. But as there are many hogs and dogs roaming at large through their villages, they are very careful to fence their dwellings round with wicker work, to preserve them from the depredations of these animals; and as the houses are extremely low, they have very much the appearance of bird cages or rabbit hutches. Their storehouses are generally placed upon poles, a few feet from the ground, and tabooed or consecrated. Great taste and ingenuity are displayed in carving and ornamenting these depositories. I made drawings from several of them, which were entirely covered with carving; and some good attempts at groups of figures, as large as life, plainly showed the dawning of the art of sculpture amongst them. Many of the attempts of the New Zealanders in that art are quite as good, if not better, than various specimens I have seen of the first efforts of the early Egyptians.

Painting and sculpture are both arts greatly admired by these rude people. Every house of consequence is ornamented and embellished, and their canoes have the most minute and elaborate workmanship bestowed upon them.

Their food is always eaten out of little baskets, rudely woven of green flax; and as they generally leave some for their next meal, they hang these baskets on sticks or props, till they are ready to eat again. Thus a village presents a very singular appearance, as it is stuck full of sticks, with various kinds of baskets hanging from them. This plan, however, is the most rational that could be adopted, as none of their eatables can be left on the ground, or they would become the prey of the hogs and dogs.

In the course of our long ramble we noticed many pretty little huts, some having neat gardens all round them, planted with fruits and corn. One house which we saw was built by a chief who had made several voyages to Port Jackson, and it was really a very comfortable dwelling. It had a high door, which we could enter without stooping, and in a separate room was constructed a bed, after the pattern of one on ship-board. He had likewise a large sea-chest in his house, the key of which (highly polished) was hung round his neck as an ornament. In the course of our walk we came to a spot on which a group of old people were sitting sunning themselves, and they immediately all rose to welcome us. I remarked one amongst them who seemed, from his silvery locks and feeble limbs, to be very old. I asked him, among other questions, whether he remembered Captain Cook. He said he did not, but well recollected Captain Furneaux, and was one of the party which cut off and massacred his boat's crew; and from other information which I received I believe his assertion to have been correct.[3]

FOOTNOTES:

[3]

Captain Furneaux's account of this massacre is printed in the Appendix.

CHAPTER IV

THE HOKIANGA RIVER EIGHTY YEARS AGO

As our missionary passengers had by this time fixed upon the spot where they intended to establish their settlement, and it being several miles up the river, we got under weigh to proceed thither. The captain's agreement being to that effect, we proceeded with the first fair wind, about twenty miles up the stream, which was as far as we could with safety take the vessel. The shores on each side this noble river are composed of hills gradually rising behind each other, most of them covered with woods to the water's edge. Not a vestige of a habitation is to be seen, and if it had not been for the occasional sight of a canoe, we might have imagined the country to be totally uninhabited. Opposite a small island, or, rather, sand-bank, the vessel grounded, and had to remain there till the next tide floated her off. It was a curious and interesting spot, being a native pa and depot, and was entirely covered with storehouses for provisions and ammunition. The centre was so contrived that all assailants might be cut off before they could effect a landing; and we were all much gratified by the judgment and forethought displayed in this little military work. The next morning we got off, but could not proceed far, as the shoals were becoming so numerous as to render the navigation dangerous. But here we beheld, with both surprise and satisfaction, a most unexpected sight, namely, a snug little colony of our own countrymen, comfortably settled and usefully employed in this savage and unexplored country. Some enterprising merchants of Port Jackson have established here a dockyard and a number of sawpits. Several vessels have been laden with timber and spars; one vessel has been built, launched, and sent to sea from this spot; and another of a hundred and fifty tons burthen was then upon the stocks!

On landing at this establishment at Te Horeke, or, as the Englishmen have called it, "Deptford," I was greatly delighted with the appearance of order, bustle, and industry it presented. Here were storehouses, dwelling-houses, and various offices for the mechanics; and every department seemed as well filled as it could have been in a civilised country. To me the most interesting circumstance was to notice the great delight of the natives, and the pleasure they seemed to take in observing the progress of the various works. All were officious to "lend a hand," and each seemed eager to be employed. This feeling corresponds with my idea of the best method of civilising a savage. Nothing can more completely show the importance of the useful arts than a dockyard. In it are practised nearly all the mechanical trades; and these present to the busy enquiring mind of a New Zealander a practical encyclopaedia of knowledge. When he sees the combined exertions of the smith and carpenter create so huge a fabric as a ship, his mind is filled with wonder and delight; and when he witnesses the moulding of iron at the anvil, it excites his astonishment and emulation.

The people of the dockyard informed me that, although it was constantly crowded with natives, scarcely anything had ever been stolen, and all the chiefs in the neighbourhood took so great an interest in the work that any annoyance offered to those employed would immediately be revenged as a personal affront.

CHAPTER V

JOURNEY OVERLAND TO BAY OF ISLANDS

Here we left the brig to unload her cargo; my friend Shand and myself having determined to proceed overland to the Bay of Islands. An intelligent chief, hearing of our intention, offered to accompany us himself, and lent us two of his kookies to carry our baggage. We accepted the chieftain's offer, and several other natives joined the party to bear us company.

November 7.—We all embarked in a canoe, in order to reach the head of the river before we began our pedestrian tour; and, after paddling about eight or nine miles further up, where the river became exceedingly narrow, we came to another English settlement. This consisted of a party of men who had come out in the Rosanna, the vessel employed by the New Zealand Company. When all ideas of settling were totally abandoned by the officers sent out for that purpose, these men chose rather to remain by themselves than to return home; and we found them busily employed in cutting timber, sawing planks, and making oars for the Sydney market. How far they may prove successful, time only can develop; but as these enterprising men had only their own industry to assist them, it could not be expected that their establishment could bear a comparison with the one at Te Horeke, which is supported by several of the most wealthy merchants of New South Wales.

As the river became narrower, the habitations of the natives were more numerous. The chief of this district (whose name is Patuone) has a splendid village very near the carpenters' establishment we have just described. He had taken these industrious men under his especial protection, and seemed very proud of having a settlement of that kind in his territories, as it gave him power and consequence among all the neighbouring chiefs, from the trade he carried on by means of their exertions.

Patuone had likewise induced the Wesleyan missionaries to settle upon his land, about a mile below; so that the head of this river assumed quite the appearance of a civilised colony.

Our party now disembarked. We landed in a dense forest, which reached to the water's edge; and our guides and slaves began to divide the loads each was to carry on his back. Several joined us from the two English stations on the river, and we then amounted to a very large party; all in high spirits, and anxious to proceed on our journey. When our natives had distributed the luggage, they loaded themselves, which they did with both skill and quickness; for a New Zealander is never at a loss for cords or ropes. Their plan is to gather a few handfuls of flax, which they soon twist into a very good substitute: with this material they formed slings, with which they dexterously fastened our moveables on their backs, and set off at a good trot, calling out to us to follow them.

CHAPTER VI

MEETING WITH THE CHIEF PATUONE

We travelled through a wood so thick that the light of heaven could not penetrate the trees that composed it. They were so large and so close together that in many places we had some difficulty to squeeze ourselves through them. To add to our perplexities, innumerable streams intersected this forest, which always brought us Europeans to a complete standstill. The only bridges which the natives ever think of making are formed by cutting down a tree, and letting it fall across; and over these our bare-legged attendants, loaded as they were, scrambled with all the agility of cats or monkeys; but it was not so with us: for several times they seated one of us on the top of their load, and carried him over. The chief, who accompanied us, made it his particular business to see me safe through every difficulty, and many times he carried me himself over such places as I dared scarcely venture to look down upon.

In the midst of this wood we met the chief of this district, Patuone, who, together with all his family, were employed in planting a small, cleared patch of land. He appeared highly delighted at beholding strangers; and all his wives came from their occupations to welcome us. He told us that, a very few miles farther on, we should come to a village belonging to him, where his eldest son was residing, and that we must there pass the night.

We thanked him for the invitation, rubbed noses with him (their token of friendship), and parted.

Soon after parting with Patuone, we fell in with a most beautiful bull, cow, and calf. I was amazed at seeing such fine animals in this country; but my companions soon cleared up the mystery by informing me that they were gifts from the missionaries, who had orders from Home to distribute these useful animals amongst such chiefs as they thought would take care of them: a wise and beneficial measure. These animals were tabooed, consequently they could ramble wherever they found food most to their liking. About dusk we arrived at the village Patuone had described to us. We were most happy to see it, as we were heartily tired, and dripping wet from a recent and heavy shower.

Patuone, a Notable Hokianga Chief.

CHAPTER VII

A MAORI VILLAGE

The village was situated on the side of a small, picturesque stream, one of the branches of the Hokianga, but continued droughts had at this time reduced it to a trifling brook. From its lofty banks, and the large trees lying athwart it, we conjectured that during heavy rains it must be a mighty flood. A long straggling collection of huts composed the village: a great deal of land in its vicinity was cleared and planted, which doubtless was the ostensible object of Patuone's people being here. As the village lay upon the opposite shore from that on which we arrived, we sat some time under the shelter of a large tree, to contemplate its appearance, and to give time to arrange our party for passing the stream, and also for my making a sketch. The red glare of the setting sun, just touching the top of every object, beautifully illuminated the landscape; and its rays bursting through the black woods in the background, gave the woods an appearance of being on fire; while a beautiful rainbow, thrown across the sky, tinged the scene with a fairy-land effect.

As soon as they perceived us from the opposite shore, a loud shout of welcome was raised, and all the inhabitants came out to meet us. They carried us over the stream, conducted us to their huts, and then sat down to gaze at and admire us.

As we were very hungry after our fatiguing walk, we soon unpacked our baggage, and in so doing made an unavoidable display of many valuable and glittering objects, which roused the attention of our savage spectators, and caused them, on the unfolding of every fresh object, to make loud and long exclamations of wonder and amazement. As I was then "a stranger in their land," and unaccustomed to their peculiarities, I felt a little alarmed at their shouts; but, on a longer acquaintance with them, I found my fears had been groundless.

Here we saw the son of Patuone, accompanied by thirty or forty young savages, sitting or lying all round us. All were exceedingly handsome, notwithstanding the wildness of their appearance and the ferocity of their looks. Let the reader picture to himself this savage group, handling everything they saw, each one armed with a musket, loaded with ball, a cartouch-box buckled round his waist, and a stone patoo-patoo, or hatchet, in his hand, while human bones were hung round each neck by way of ornament; let the scene and situation be taken into consideration, and he will acknowledge it was calculated to make the young traveller wish himself safe at home; but, when I suspected, I wronged them; for after admiring everything we had brought with us (more especially our fowling-pieces, which were very beautiful ones), they begged a little tobacco, then retired to a distance from the hut which had been prepared for our reception, and left us to take our supper uninterrupted; after which they placed all our baggage in the hut, that we might be assured of its safety.

It proved a rainy, miserable night; and we were a large party, crowded into a small, smoky hut, with a fire lighted in the middle; as, after our supper, the natives, in order to have as much of our company as possible, crowded it till it was literally crammed. However annoying this might be, still I was recompensed by the novelty and picturesque appearance of the scene. Salvator Rosa could not have conceived a finer study of the horrible. A dozen men, of the largest and most athletic forms, their cakahoos (or mat-dresses) laid aside, and their huge limbs exposed to the red glare of the fire; their faces rendered hideous by being tattooed all over, showing by the firelight quite a bright blue; their eyes, which are remarkable for their fierce expression, all fixed upon us, but with a look of good temper, co-mingled with intense curiosity. All my fears had by this time subsided, and, being master of myself, I had leisure to study and enjoy the scene; we smoked a social pipe with them (for they are all immoderately fond of tobacco), and I then stretched myself down to sleep amidst all their chattering and smoke.

But all my attempts at slumber were fruitless. I underwent a simultaneous attack of vermin of all descriptions; fleas, mosquitoes, and sand-flies, which, beside their depredations on my person, made such a buzzing noise, that even the chattering of the natives could not drown it, or the smoke from the fire or pipes drive them away.

CHAPTER VIII

TOILSOME JOURNEY THROUGH THE FOREST

Next morning, at daybreak, we took leave of our hosts, and proceeded on our journey; we had eight miles more of this thick forest to scramble through, and this part we found considerably worse than that we had traversed yesterday. The roots of trees covered the path in all directions, rendering it necessary to watch every step we took, in order to prevent being thrown down; the supple-jacks, suspended and twining from tree to tree, making in many places a complete net-work; and while we were toiling with the greatest difficulty through this miserable road, our natives were jogging on as comfortably as possible: use had so completely accustomed them to it, that they sprung over the roots, and dived under the supple-jacks and branches, with perfect ease, while we were panting after them in vain. The whole way was mountainous. The climbing up, and then descending, was truly frightful; not a gleam of sky was to be seen, all was a mass of gigantic trees, straight and lofty, their wide spreading branches mingling overhead, and producing throughout the forest an endless darkness and unbroken gloom.

After three or four hours of laborious struggling, we emerged from the wood, and found ourselves upon an extensive plain, which, as far as the eye could reach, appeared covered with fern. A small path lay before us, and this was our road. The New Zealanders always travel on foot, one after the other, or in Indian file. Their pathways are not more than a foot wide, which to a European is most painful; but as the natives invariably walk with the feet turned in, or pigeon-toed, they feel no inconvenience from the narrowness. When a traveller is once on the path, it is impossible for him to go astray. No other animal, except man, ever traverses this country, and *his* track cannot be mistaken, since none ever deviate from the beaten footpath, which was in consequence, in some places (where the soil was light), worn so deep as to resemble a gutter more than a road.

We proceeded for many miles in this unsocial manner; unsocial, for it precludes all conversation. Our natives occasionally gave us a song, or, rather, dirge, in which they all joined chorus. Having at length attained the summit of a hill, we beheld the Bay of Islands, stretching out in the distance; and at sunset we arrived at the Kerikeri river, where there is a Church-missionary settlement.

Mission Station, Kerikeri.

CHAPTER IX

THE MISSIONARY SETTLEMENT AT KERIKERI

We had travelled all day through a country in which every object we saw was of a character that reminded us forcibly of the savage community we were with. Occasionally we met groups of naked men, trotting along under immense loads, and screaming their barbarous songs of recognition; sometimes we beheld an uncouthly carved figure, daubed over with red ochre, and fixed in the ground, to give notice that one side of the road was tabooed. An extraordinary contrast was now presented to our view, for we came suddenly in front of a complete little English village. Wreaths of white smoke were rising from the chimneys, of neat weather-boarded houses. The glazed windows reflected the brilliant glow from the rays of the setting sun, while herds of fat cattle were winding down the hills, lowing as they leisurely bent their steps toward the farm-yard. It is impossible for me to describe what I felt on contemplating a scene so similar to those I had left behind me.

According to the custom of this country, we fired our muskets, to warn the inhabitants of the settlement of our approach. We arranged our dresses in the best order we could, and proceeded towards the village. As the report of our guns had been heard, groups of nondescripts came running out to meet us. I could scarcely tell to what order of beings they belonged; but on their near approach, I found them to be the New Zealand youths, who were settled with the missionaries. They were habited in the most uncouth dresses imaginable. These pious men, certainly, have no taste for the picturesque; they had obscured the finest human forms under a seaman's huge clothing. Boys not more than fifteen wore jackets reaching to their knees, and buttoned up to the throat with great black horn buttons, a coarse checked shirt, the collar of which spread half-way over their face, their luxuriant, beautiful hair was cut close off, and each head was crammed into a close Scotch bonnet!

These half-converted, or, rather, half-*covered*, youths, after rubbing noses, and chattering with our guides, conducted us to the dwellings of their masters. As I had a letter of introduction from one of their own body, I felt not the slightest doubt of a kind reception; so we proceeded with confidence. We were ushered into a house, all cleanliness and comfort, all order, silence, and unsociability. After presenting my letter to a grave-looking personage, it had to undergo a private inspection in an adjoining room, and the result was an invitation "to stay and take a cup of tea!" All that an abundant farm and excellent grocer in England could supply were soon before us. Each person of the mission, as he appeared during our repast, was called aside, and I could hear my own letter read and discussed by them. I could not help thinking (within myself) whether this was a way to receive a countryman at the Antipodes! No smile beamed upon their countenance; there were no inquiries after news; in short, there was no touch of human sympathy, such as we "of the world" feel at receiving an Englishman under our roof in such a savage country as this!

The chubby children who peeped at us from all corners, and the very hearty appearance of their parents, plainly evidenced that theirs was an excellent and thriving trade. We had a cold invitation to stay all night; but this the number of our party entirely precluded; so they lent us their boat to convey us to the Bay of Islands, a distance of about twenty-five miles.

As the night proved dark and stormy, and as our boat was crowded with natives, our passage down the Kerikeri river became both disagreeable and dangerous. The river being filled with rocks, some under, and others just above the water, we were obliged to keep a good look-out. After experiencing many alarms, we arrived safely at Kororareka beach about midnight, where an Englishman of the name of Johnstone gave us a shelter in his hut.

CHAPTER X

THE BAY OF ISLANDS

In the morning we beheld two vessels at anchor in the harbour. The Indian, whaler, of London, and the East India Company's ship Research; which latter ship had been cruising in search of the wreck of the vessels under the command of La Perouse, and had completely elucidated the circumstances relating to that event. The Bay of Islands is surrounded by lofty and picturesque hills, and is secured from all winds. It is full of lovely coves, and a safe anchorage is to be found nearly all over it; added to this, a number of navigable rivers are for ever emptying themselves into the Bay, which is spotted with innumerable romantic islands all covered with perpetual verdure.

It is with peculiar interest that we look upon the spot where the illustrious Cook cast anchor after his discovery of this Bay. Some unhappy quarrels with the natives occasioned much blood to be shed on both sides, and for a long time caused this island to be looked upon with horror, and avoided by all Europeans. It was the courage and enterprise of the crews of our South Sea Whalers who exhibited these interesting islanders in their true character, and proved to the world that it was quite as safe to anchor in the Bay of Islands as in the harbour of Port Jackson.

CHAPTER XI

THE MASSACRE OF THE "BOYD"

Since the time of Cook, and other circumnavigators of that period, the character of these people has undergone a thorough change. Then it was necessary when a ship anchored, that the boarding nettings should be up, and all the arms ready for immediate use. The principal object the chiefs had in view seemed to be to lull the commanders into a fatal security, then to rush upon them, seize their vessel, and murder all the crew! Too often had they succeeded, and as often have they paid most dearly for their treachery and cruelty. In the case of the ship Boyd, though they attained their object, they were as completely punished for their perfidy. From their ignorance of the nature of powder, and the use of a magazine, they blew up the ship, and vast numbers of the natives were destroyed. Besides this calamity, they brought down upon themselves the vengeance of every vessel that visited these shores for a long period afterwards. As the circumstances may not be generally known, Mr. Berry's letter, relating the particulars of that melancholy, yet interesting event, is here inserted:—

"Ship, City of Edinburgh,
"Lima, Oct. 20, 1810.

Sir,—

I am very sorry to have the painful task of introducing myself to you, with an account of the loss of your ship Boyd, Captain Thompson.

Towards the end of last year I was employed in the Bay of Islands, New Zealand, in procuring a cargo of spars for the Cape of Good Hope. About the middle of December the natives brought me an account of a ship's being taken at Whangaroa, a harbour about fifty miles to the N.W. At first we were disposed to doubt the truth of this report, but it every day became more probable, from the variety of circumstances they informed us of; and which were so connected as appeared impossible for them to invent. Accordingly, about the end of the month, when we had finished our cargo, although it was a business of some danger, I determined to go round.

"I set out with three armed boats: we experienced very bad weather, and after a narrow escape were glad to return to the ship. As we arrived in a most miserable condition, I had then relinquished all idea of the enterprise; but having recruited my strength and spirits, I was shocked at the idea of leaving any of my countrymen in the hands of savages, and determined to make a second attempt. We had this time better weather, and reached the harbour without any difficulty. Whangaroa is formed as follows:—First, a large outer bay, with an island at its entrance; in the bottom of this bay is seen a narrow opening, which appears terminated at the distance of a quarter of a mile; but, upon entering it, it is seen to expand into two large basins, at least as secure as any of the docks on the banks of the Thames, and capable of containing (I think) the whole British navy. We found the wreck of the Boyd in shoal water, at the top of the harbour, a most melancholy picture of wanton mischief. The natives had cut her cables, and towed her up the harbour till she had grounded, and then set her on fire, and burnt her to the water's edge. In her hold were seen the remains of her cargo— coals, salted seal skins, and planks. Her guns, iron, standards, etc., were lying on the top, having fallen in when her decks were consumed.

"The cargo must have been very valuable; but it appears that the captain, anxious to make a better voyage, had come to that port for the purpose of filling up with spars for the Cape of Good Hope.

"Not to tire you with the minutia of the business, I recovered from the natives a woman, two children, and a boy of the name of Davies, one of your apprentices, who were the only survivors. I found also the accompanying papers, which, I hope, may prove of service to you. I did all this by gentle measures, and you will admit that bloodshed and revenge would have answered no good purpose. The ship was taken the third morning after her arrival. The captain had been rather too hasty in resenting some slight theft. Early in the morning the ship was surrounded by a great number of canoes, and many natives gradually insinuated themselves on board. Tippahee, a chief of the Bay of Islands, and who had been twice at Port Jackson, also arrived; he went into the cabin, and, after paying his respects to the captain, begged a little bread for his men; but the captain received him rather slightingly, and desired him to go away, and not trouble him, as he was busy.

"The proud old savage (who had been a constant guest at the Governor's table at Port Jackson) was highly offended at this treatment, immediately left the cabin, and, after stamping a few minutes on the deck, went into his canoe. After breakfast the captain went on shore with four hands, and no other arms but his fowling-piece. From the account of the savages, as soon as he landed they rushed upon him; he had only time to fire his piece, and it killed a child. As soon as the captain left the ship, Tippahee (who remained alongside in his canoe) came again on board. A number of sailors were repairing sails upon the quarter deck, and the remainder were carelessly dispersed about, and fifty of the natives were sitting on the deck. In a moment they all started up, and each knocked his man on the head: a few ran wounded below, and four or five escaped up the rigging, and in a few seconds the savages had complete possession of the ship. The boy Davies escaped into the hold, where he lay concealed for several days, till they were fairly glutted with human blood, when they spared his life. The woman says she was discovered by an old savage, and that she moved him by her tears and embraces; that he (being a subordinate chief) carried her to Tippahee, who allowed him to spare her life. She says, that at this time the deck was covered with human bodies, which they were employed in cutting up; after which they exhibited a most horrid dance and song in honour of their victory, and concluded by a hymn of gratitude to their god.

"Tippahee now took the speaking trumpet, and hailing the poor wretches at the mast-head, told them that he was now captain, and that they must in future obey his commands. He then ordered them to unbend the sails, they readily complied; but when he ordered them to come down they hesitated, but he enforced prompt obedience by threatening to cut away the masts. When they came down he received them with much civility, and told them he would take care of them; he immediately ordered them into a canoe, and sent them on shore. A few minutes after this the woman went on shore with her deliverer. The first object that struck her view was the dead bodies of these men, lying naked on the beach. As soon as she landed a number of men started up, and marched towards her with their patoo-patoos. A number of women ran screaming betwixt them, covered her with their clothes, and by tears and entreaties saved her life.

"The horrid feasting on human flesh which followed would be too shocking for description. The second mate begged his life at the time of the general massacre; they spared him for a fortnight, and then killed and eat him. I think if the captain had received Tippahee with a little more civility, that he would have informed him of his danger, and saved the ship; but that from being treated in the manner I have mentioned, he entered into the plot along with the others.

"I assure you it has been a most unpleasant thing for me to write about, and I could only have been induced to do it from a sense of duty, and a desire to give you all the information in my power, which I suppose may be of some use.

"I am, Sir,
"Your obedient humble servant,
"ALEXANDER BERRY."

Considering Mr. Berry's limited acquaintance with these islanders, and the horror of the scene before him, his is a good and an impartial account; but facts which have been obtained subsequently have exonerated the natives to a certain extent. By repeated conversations I have held with several chiefs who were engaged in this dreadful affair, and from information I procured at Sydney, I have no doubt but that the Captain himself was the most in fault.

Whangaroa, Scene of the "Boyd" Massacre.

He was commissioned by the Government of New South Wales to land a native chief named Philip at New Zealand, whom he subjected to a cruel and impolitic punishment. This man, smarting from his stripes, and burning with a desire to revenge his dishonourable treatment, excited all his friends to the commission of that bloody massacre.

CHAPTER XII

THE FIRST SETTLEMENT AT KORORAREKA

The tragic fate of the Boyd's crew is now fast sinking into oblivion; and, like the islanders of Hawaii, after the murder of Cook, they seem to wish to obliterate the remembrance of their disgraceful conduct by a kind and friendly intercourse with our nation. The severe chastisement which they have always received from us after a treacherous action, has proved to them how little they gain by so debasing a line of conduct; and as they are most anxious to possess many of our productions, they seem to have come to a resolution to abandon their former system; which, if they may not be sensible of the injustice of, they see is destructive to their own interests; and now every chief is as solicitous for the safety of a European vessel as he would have been formerly for its destruction.

They have not only lost a portion of their ferocity, but also much of their native simplicity of character, which, in all parts of the world, is so highly interesting a study for the traveller. Their constant intercourse with whalers, who are generally low, unpolished men, leaves behind it a tinge of vulgarity, of which the native women retain the largest portion. In many instances, they quite spoil their good looks, by half adopting the European costume. Those who are living in the retirement of their own villages have a natural ease and elegance of manner, which they soon lose after their introduction to our rough sailors. I have seen a party of very handsome girls, just landing from one of the whalers, their beautiful forms hid under old greasy red or checked shirts, generally put on with the hind parts before. In some cases the sailors, knowing their taste for finery, bring out with them, from London, old tawdry gowns, and fierce coloured ribands. And thus equipped, they come on shore the most grotesque objects imaginable, each highly delighted with her gaudy habiliments.

Kororareka beach, where we took up our residence, seemed the general place of rendezvous for all Europeans whom chance might bring into this bay. At this time there were two large vessels lying at anchor within a quarter of a mile of the shore, and I was informed there were sometimes as many as twelve or thirteen.

The spot is a most delightful one, being about three-quarters of a mile in extent, sheltered by two picturesque promontories, and possessing a fine circular, firm, sandy beach, on which there is seldom much surf, so that boats can at all times land and haul up. Scattered amongst the rushes and small bushes is seen a New Zealand village, which at first landing is scarcely perceptible, the huts being so low. Some of them are of English design, though of native workmanship. These are generally the dwellings of some Europeans, who are of so doubtful a character that it would be difficult to guess to what order of society they belonged previous to their being transplanted amongst these savages.

I found a respectable body of Scotch mechanics settled here, who came out in the New Zealand Company's ship Rosanna, and who determined to remain at Kororareka. Their persevering industry as yet has been crowned with success, and they seem well pleased with the prospects before them.

Here, these hardy sons of Britain are employed in both carrying on and instructing the wondering savage in various branches of useful art. Here the smith has erected his forge, and his sooty mansion is crowded by curious natives, who voluntarily perform the hardest and most dirty work, and consider themselves fully recompensed by a sight of his mysterious labours, every portion of which fills them with astonishment. Here is heard daily the sound of the sawpit, while piles of neat white planks appear arranged on the beach. These laborious and useful Scotchmen interfere with no one, and pursue successfully their industrious career, without either requiring or receiving any assistance from Home.

But there is another class of Europeans here, who are both useless and dangerous, and these lower the character of the white people in the estimation of the natives. These men are called "Beach Rangers," most of whom have deserted from, or have been turned out of whalers for crimes, for which, had they been taken Home and tried, they would have been hanged; some few among them, having been too lazy to finish the voyage they had begun, had deserted from their ships, and were then leading a mean and miserable life amongst the natives.

There is still a third class of our countrymen to be met with here, whose downcast and sneaking looks proclaim them to be runaway convicts from New South Wales. These unhappy men are treated with derision and contempt by all classes; and the New Zealanders, being perfectly aware of their state of degradation, refuse all intercourse with them. They are idle, unprincipled, and vicious in the extreme, and are much feared in the Bay of Islands; for when by any means they obtain liquor, they prove themselves most dangerous neighbours.

My friend Shand and myself were most comfortably situated. An intimate friend of mine (Captain Duke, of the whaler The Sisters) had, in consequence of ill-health, taken up his residence on shore while his vessel completed her cruise. In his hut we found comfort and safety; and from his information and advice we were enabled to avoid the advances of all whom his experience had taught him were to be shunned.

On terms of the closest intimacy, and with his hut adjoining that of my friend Captain Duke, lived Shulitea[4] (or King George, as he styled himself), a chief of great power, who controlled the whole of the district where we were. We all felt grateful to him for his manifestations of friendship, and at the same time were conscious of enjoying a greater degree of security by his proximity. He was the first chief who offered protection to "the white people," and he has never been known to have broken his engagement. An unexpected and remarkable instance of his adherence to their interests, in spite of temptation, took place a few years since, which I deem worthy of relation here.

The ship Brompton, in endeavouring to work out of the bay, by some accident got on shore, and finally became a complete wreck. This fine vessel, with a valuable cargo on board, lay helpless on the beach, and the crew and passengers expected nothing less than plunder and destruction. The natives from the interior, hearing of the circumstance, hastened down in vast numbers to participate in the general pillage. But King George summoned all his warriors to his aid, and with this party placed himself between the wreck and those who came to plunder it. I was informed by several who were present at the time, that, after declaring that "not an article should be taken till himself and all his party were destroyed," he advanced, and thus explained his reasons for protecting the strangers and their property:—

"You" (said King George) "come from the interior; all of you think only of what you can get, without considering the consequences, which, indeed, are of little import to you, living, as you do, out of reach of the reproaches and vengeance of the white men. But look how differently I am situated. I live on the beach; this Bay is my residence; I invite the white men to come and trade here under the promise of my protection; they come; several years of profitable trading have passed between us. King George, they say, is a good man; now an accident has befallen one of their ships in my territory, what must King George do? Why, he *must* assist them; which he *will* do, and defend them against everyone who shall attempt to injure them." In consequence of this speech, and his exertions, not a thing was taken from the wreck by the savages who had collected for that purpose.

FOOTNOTES:

[4]

The chief referred to by Mr. Earle as Shulitea, or King George, was a noted Bay of Islands chief named Whareumu. He was killed in a fight with the Hokianga tribes, in March, 1828. (See appendix.)

CHAPTER XIII

MAORI NON-PROGRESSIVENESS

This anecdote proves that King George and his people possessed feelings of honour and generosity, which, if properly cultivated, might lead to the most happy results. From the length of time these people have been known to the Europeans, it might naturally be expected that great changes would have taken place in their habits, manners, arts, and manufactures; but this is not the case. Their huts are of the same diminutive proportions as described by Captain Cook; their clothing and mats, their canoes and paddles, are precisely the same as when that navigator described them. When they can obtain English tools, they use them in preference to their own; still their work is not better done. The only material change that has taken place is in their mode of warfare.

The moment the New Zealanders became acquainted with the nature of firearms, their minds were directed but to one point, namely, to become possessed of them. After many ingenious and treacherous attempts to obtain these oft-coveted treasures, and which, for the most part, ended in their defeat, they had recourse to industry, and determined to create commodities which they might fairly barter for these envied muskets. Potatoes were planted, hogs were reared, and flax prepared, not for their own use or comfort, but to exchange with the Europeans for firearms. Their plans succeeded; and they have now fairly possessed themselves of those weapons, which at first made us so formidable in their eyes; and as they are in constant want of fresh supplies of ammunition, I feel convinced it will always be their wish to be on friendly terms with us, for the purpose of procuring these desirable stores. I have not heard of a single instance in which they have turned these arms against us, though they are often grossly insulted.

In their combats with each other, firearms are used with dreadful effect. The whole soul of a New Zealander seems absorbed in the thoughts of war; every action of his life is influenced by it; and to possess weapons which give him such a decided superiority over those who have only their native implements of offence, he will sacrifice everything. The value attached by them to muskets, and their ceaseless desire to possess them, will prove a sufficient security to foreigners who enter their harbours, or remain on their coasts; as I know, from experience, that the New Zealanders will rather put up with injuries than run the risk of offending those who manufacture and barter with them such inestimable commodities.

CHAPTER XIV

A MISSION SETTLEMENT

A few days after my arrival in the Bay, I crossed to the opposite side, to visit the Church missionary settlement, and to deliver a letter of introduction I had to one of the members. Here, on a beautiful bank, with a delightful beach in front, and the entrance of the bay open to them, the clear and blue expanse of water speckled over with fertile islands, reside these comfortable teachers of the Gospel. The name they have given this spot is "Marsden Vale." They very soon gave us to understand they did not wish for our acquaintance, and their coldness and inhospitality (I must acknowledge) created in my mind a thorough dislike to them. The object of the mission, as it was first planned, might have been attained, and might have proved highly beneficial to the New Zealanders; but as it is now conducted, no good result can be expected from it. Any man of common sense must agree with me, that a savage can receive but little benefit from having the abstruse points of the Gospel preached to him, if his mind is not prepared to receive them. This is the plan adopted here; and nothing will convince these enthusiasts that it is wrong, or induce them to change it for one more agreeable to the dictates of reason.

Upon inquiring who and what these men were, I found that the greater part of them were hardy mechanics (not well-educated clergymen), whom the benevolent and well-intentioned people of England had sent out in order to teach the natives the importance of *different trades*—a most judicious arrangement, and which ought to be the foundation of all missions. What could be a more gratifying sight than groups of these athletic savages, toiling at the anvil or the saw; erecting for themselves substantial dwellings; thus leading them by degrees to know and to appreciate the comforts resulting from peaceful, laborious, and useful occupations? Then, while they felt sincere gratitude for services rendered them, at their leisure hours, and on certain days, *these* missionaries should attempt to expound to them, in as simple a manner as possible, the nature of revealed religion!

In New Zealand, the "mechanic" missionary only carries on his trade till he has every comfort around him—his house finished, his garden fenced, and a strong stockade enclosing all, to keep off the "pagan" savages. This done, then commences the easy task of preaching. They collect a few ragged urchins of natives, whom they teach to read and write their own language—the English tongue being forbidden; and when these children return to their families, they are despised by them, as being effeminate and useless.

I once saw a sturdy blacksmith in the prime of life, sitting in the midst of a group of savages, attempting to expound to them the mysteries of our holy redemption—perplexing his own brains, as well as those of his auditors, with the most incomprehensible and absurd opinions. How much better would he have been employed in teaching them how to weld a piece of iron, or to make a nail!

What causes much disapprobation here, is the contemptuous manner in which they treat their own countrymen, as they receive most of them on the outside of their stockade fence.

On our return from Marsden Vale, our savage friends laughed heartily at us. They had warned us of the reception we should meet with; and their delight at seeing us again formed a strange contrast to that of their Christian teachers, whose inhospitable dwellings we determined never to reenter.

CHAPTER XV

A VISIT FROM HONGI

A few days after my visit to the missionaries, while we were busily employed in constructing our huts, assisted by about fifty natives, on a sudden a great commotion took place amongst them. Each left his work and ran to his hut, and immediately returned armed with both musket and cartouch box: apparently all the arms in the village were mustered, and all seemed ready for immediate use. On inquiring into the cause of all these war-like preparations, I was informed that Hongi and his chief men were crossing the bay in several large war canoes; and though he was considered as a friend and ally, yet, as he was a man of such desperate ambition, and consummate cunning, it was considered necessary to receive him under arms, which he might take either as a compliment, or as a proof of how well they were aware of the guest they were receiving.

This man, Hongi, was a most extraordinary character, and a person I had long had a great curiosity to see, his daring and savage deeds having often been the subject of conversation in New South Wales. In his own country he was looked upon as invulnerable and invincible. In the year 1821 he had visited England, during which he had been honoured by having a personal interview with George the Fourth, and had received from His Majesty several valuable presents; amongst others, were a superb suit of chain armour, and a splendid double-barrelled gun. From possessing these arms, so far superior to any of his neighbours, he looked upon himself as impossible to be conquered, and commenced a career of warfare and destruction on all his enemies, and nearly exterminated them. His friends called him "a god," and his enemies feared him as "a devil." Last year, Hongi made war upon, and totally annihilated, the tribe who had fifteen years previously attacked and murdered the crew of the Boyd. He had long determined to take revenge for that treacherous action, as he always styled himself "the friend of the English." After this, he removed his residence, and took possession of the conquered district. But in this his last battle he had to fight without his invulnerable coat of mail, his slaves having stolen it and gone over with it to the enemy. His people were now confirmed in their superstition respecting its being proof against shot, by his having received during the combat a bullet in the breast, from the effects of which he is fast sinking into the grave. His companions related the following extraordinary anecdote concerning him after he received this wound, which proves his great presence of mind.

His party were retreating, and the enemy were charging him vigorously; Hongi stood alone when he received the bullet; he did not fall immediately, and the enemy were eagerly running up to despatch him, when he roused all his energies, and shouted aloud for the two hundred chiefs, who lay concealed, to rush forward and fall on. The foe, hearing this, paused, when about a dozen chiefs, and indeed, as Hongi well knew, all that he had, suddenly made their appearance. This caused a panic; they turned about; the pursued became the pursuers, and nearly the whole tribe were destroyed.

CHAPTER XVI

INTERVIEW WITH THE GREAT MAORI CONQUEROR

He landed about a mile from the village, and we lost no time in procuring an interpreter, with whom we went instantly to pay our respects to this celebrated conqueror.

We found him and his party; his slaves preparing their morning repast. The scene altogether was highly interesting. In a beautiful bay, surrounded by high rocks and overhanging trees, the chiefs sat in mute contemplation, their arms piled up in regular order on the beach. Hongi, not only from his high rank (but in consequence of his wound being toboo'd, or rendered holy), sat apart from the rest. Their richly ornamented war canoes were drawn up on the strand; some of the slaves were unlading stores, others were kindling fires. To me it almost seemed to realise some of the passages of Homer, where he describes the wanderer Ulysses and his gallant band of warriors. We approached the chief, and paid our respects to him. He received us kindly, and with a dignified composure, as one accustomed to receive homage. His look was emaciated; but so mild was the expression of his features, that he would have been the last man I should have imagined accustomed to scenes of bloodshed and cruelty. But I soon remarked, that when he became animated in conversation, his eyes sparkled with fire, and their expression changed, demonstrating that it only required his passions to be roused to exhibit him under a very different aspect. His wife and daughter were permitted to sit close to him, to administer to his wants, no others being allowed so to do, on account of his taboo.

He was arrayed in a new blanket, which completely enveloped his figure, leaving exposed his highly-tattooed face, and head profusely covered with long, black, curling hair, adorned with a quantity of white feathers. He was altogether a very fine study; and, with his permission, I made a sketch of him, and also one including the whole group. Finding we were newcomers, he asked us a variety of questions, and, among others, our opinion of his country. His remarks were judicious and sensible, and he seemed much pleased with our admiration of his territory. I produced a bottle of wine that I had brought with me, and his wife supplied him with a few glasses, which seemed to revive and animate him.

We were then invited to join him in a trip in one of his canoes, in which was placed a bed for him to recline upon; his wife seated herself close to him, while his daughter, a very pretty, interesting girl about fifteen years of age, took a paddle in her hand, which she used with the greatest dexterity. I took the liberty of presenting her with a bracelet, with which she seemed highly delighted; when Hongi, perceiving that I was in a giving mood, pointed to his beard, and asked me for a razor. Fortunately, I had put one in my pocket on setting out, and I now presented it to him, by which gifts we continued on terms of great sociability and friendship. After a pleasant cruise with this (to us) extraordinary family, and contriving to make ourselves pretty well understood, we returned about the close of the day, and landed at the bay. All the natives were much delighted at our confidence in them, and we were equally gratified by their hospitality.

CHAPTER XVII

A MAORI WELCOME

I was much amused with the punctilios used in the visit of ceremony paid to King George. Hongi, accompanied by about a dozen of his chiefs, advanced towards our settlement, leaving their guns and hatchets behind them; as they approached, all our tribe discharged their pieces in the air. When they met, all rubbed noses (a ceremony never to be dispensed with on formal occasions). They were then conducted by King George to his huts on the beach, and in the enclosure in front of them the warriors squatted on the ground. Hongi, being tabooed, or under the immediate protection of their Atua, or God, still sat apart. Then the mother of George, called Tururo, or the Queen, and who is regarded quite as a sybil by the whole tribe, approached Hongi with the greatest respect and caution, and seated herself some paces from his feet. She then began, with a most melancholy cadence (her eyes streaming with tears and fixed upon the ground), the song of welcome. All their meetings of ceremony or friendship begin with the shedding of copious floods of tears; and as Hongi's visit was such an unhoped for and unexpected honour, so much greater in proportion was the necessity for their lamentations. This woeful song lasted half an hour, and all the assembly were soon in tears; and though at first I was inclined to turn it into ridicule, I was soon in the same state myself. The pathetic strain, and the scene altogether, was most impressive. As the song proceeded, I was informed of the nature of the subject, which was a theme highly calculated to affect all present. She began by complimenting the wounded warrior, deploring the incurable state of his wound, and regretting that God was wanting him, and was about so soon to take him from his friends! Then she recounted some of his most celebrated deeds of valour, naming and deploring the number of his friends who had fallen bravely in the wars, and lamenting that the enemies who had killed them were still living! This part seemed to affect them powerfully; and when Tururo ceased her song (being quite exhausted) they all rose, thus demonstrating their respect and approbation.

This was followed by a general attack upon the good things King George had prepared for them. The slaves came flocking in, bearing baskets of hot kumaras, potatoes, and fish. I observed their tears had not spoiled their appetites; they ate voraciously. After having done great honour to the feast, they all started on their feet for a dance, which lasted a long while, and with which they concluded the evening.

The dances of all savage nations are beautiful, but those of the New Zealanders partake also of the horrible. The regularity of their movements is truly astonishing; and the song, which always accompanies a dance, is most harmonious. They soon work themselves up to a pitch of frenzy; the distortions of their face and body are truly dreadful, and fill the mind with horror. Love and war are the subjects of their songs and dances; but the details of the latter passion are by far the most popular among them. I was astonished to find that their women mixed in the dance indiscriminately with the men, and went through all those horrid gestures with seemingly as much pleasure as the warriors themselves.

The next morning I was awakened, at daybreak, by the most dismal sounds I had ever heard. I started up, and found it proceeded from the tribes parting with each other. They had divided themselves into little parties, each forming a circle, and were crying most piteously, and cutting their flesh as a cook would score pork for roasting. On such occasions each is armed with a sharp shell, or, if he can possibly obtain so valuable a prize, a piece of a broken glass bottle. All were streaming with tears and blood, while Hongi and his friends embarked in their large and richly-ornamented canoes, and sailed from our beach. After his departure, I soon discovered that, notwithstanding their apparent affection, King George and his friends were most happy their visitors had left them; and that it was more the dread of Hongi's power, than love for him, that induced them to treat him with such respect and homage.

CHAPTER XVIII

EXCURSIONS IN THE INTERIOR

I made several excursions into the interior, and each confirmed me in the good opinion I had formed of the natives. I felt myself quite safe amongst them. There is a great peculiarity in rambling through this country; namely, the total absence of quadrupeds. There are abundance of birds, which are so numerous at times as almost to darken the air—many of them possessing very sweet notes; and wild ducks, teal, etc., cover the various streams. Wherever I went I did not discover any grass, almost every part being covered either with fern or flax; the former yielding the natives their principal article of food, and the latter their clothing. To this dearth of animals may be attributed the chief cause of their ferocity and propensity to cannibalism.

In most uncivilised countries the natives use their arms against the wild animals of the forest. The dangers and difficulties they encounter in overcoming them form a kind of prelude to war, and perfect them in the use of their weapons. The rifle of the North American Indian would never be so much dreaded did he not depend upon its produce for his subsistence. I have myself (during my travels through North America) had many opportunities of witnessing the certain aim they take both with the arrow and the bullet; while those in the southern parts of that vast continent, who depend on taking the wild cattle, acquire, by constant practice, an equal dexterity with the *lassoo*, which those who have not witnessed it could scarcely imagine possible. The New Zealander, while handling a musket, is quite in a state of trepidation; and though it is his darling weapon he seems always afraid of it, and is never sure of his aim till he is quite close to his object. I have mentioned this fact to several Europeans who had accompanied various tribes to battle, and they all informed me they made a sad bungling use of the musket; their aim would be surer if they had large and ferocious animals to hunt or contend with. There is another circumstance that operates against their acquiring skill in the use of the gun: they are so fond of cleaning, scrubbing, and taking them to pieces, that in a short time the locks become loose, the screws are injured, and they are soon rendered entirely useless, to the great surprise and dismay of their owners, who are constantly pestering the Europeans by bringing them *sick* muskets (as they call them) to look at, and put to rights, and are quite surprised that we "cannot make them well again." They cannot be made to comprehend that every white man does not know how to make a musket, or, at least, to repair it.

CHAPTER XIX

ENTERTAINED BY MAORI WOMEN

On the 24th November we took our departure from the bay, as we had to return to Hokianga, where we had left our brig; and it was only under a promise of making a speedy return, and remaining longer with them, that our savage friends would suffer us to leave them. We expected to reach the Kerikeri River before night; but in this we were disappointed. It at length became quite dark; and the ebb tide making against us, rendered further advance impossible. We had to seek some place of shelter for the night, and not a hut was visible. While we were debating on what was best to be done, we observed a light from the shore, and made for it; but, it being low water, our boat stuck fast in the slime long before we reached the banks; we were, consequently, obliged to wade knee-deep through the slippery mud. We soon discovered a party of women sitting round a fire made in the midst of the swamp. They had come here for the purpose of procuring shell-fish; and as they are never very fastidious about shelter or dry beds, they had determined (according to their usual custom) to pass the night where they had been occupied during the day. This sort of bivouac I found excessively uncomfortable. The moment we were seated the water began to ooze out an inch or two all round us. We sought in vain for a dry place, for we were enveloped in darkness, and surrounded by rushes and flags six or seven feet high; but, being very much fatigued, we slept, notwithstanding the misery of a wet bed, with a cloud of fog for curtains. I did not wake till one of the women gave me a good shake, and informed me that the day was well up. They had prepared us a breakfast of hot shell-fish, which they had caught the preceding day, and they all seemed delighted by our eating heartily of them. As we had some biscuits in our boat, we sent for them, and gave our "fair founders of the feast" a share; and we were all very sociable and merry. When we left them, as it was again low water, the women carried us to our boat, and took their leave of us amidst peals of laughter. This was another proof to me that the English are quite safe, though travelling unguarded, amongst these people.

CHAPTER XX

LOADING SPARS AT HOKIANGA

About nine the next morning we reached the Kerikeri River; and, it being Sunday, the members of the mission met us on landing, and used all their endeavours to prevent our travelling on that day; but, independent of the urgent necessity of our reaching Hokianga, the captain of our vessel, who was with us, being particularly anxious to return on board, we continued our journey, and at night came to a bivouac in a dense wood, so that we now had the luxury of stretching our weary limbs on dry ground. The next day, as we journeyed towards the river, we fell in with all our old friends, who inquired into the particulars of our adventures, and seemed highly delighted at our return.

We found "all right" on board the brig; but as she was chartered to go to Tongataboo I and my friend Shand determined to remain at New Zealand till her return. Our principal difficulty seemed to be which side of the island we should make choice of for a dwelling-place. When it became known to the natives that we intended to remain with them, several chiefs came and offered us their protection; and each would have built us a house, but we preferred making our sojourn at the Bay of Islands. We were often at a loss how to evade the kind importunities of our savage hosts without giving them offence. "Is not our country as good as theirs?" —"Are you not as safe amongst us?" —"Are we not as willing and as capable of protecting you as Shulitea?" These were the arguments they used; and, finally, we were obliged to inform them that we had a friend and countryman (Captain Duke) settled on the other side, who was preparing a house for our reception. On being informed of this circumstance they consented to part with us, though evidently with great reluctance.

While we lay here the ship Harmony, of London, Captain Middleton, arrived from Sydney for a cargo of spars. So large a vessel entering the port put the whole district into commotion; and when the chiefs understood the nature of her wants, and had seen the fine double-barrelled guns and store of powder to be given as payment for the wished-for freight, they hastened to the woods, and the axe was soon laid to the roots of the trees. I saw them pursuing their laborious employ with alacrity. In a few days a sufficient number of fine logs came floating down the river to load the ship, and they were all cleared in a workmanlike manner, ready to stow away. The chief things to induce these people to work are firearms and powder; these are two stimulants to their industry which never fail.

CHAPTER XXI

DEATH OF A GREAT CHIEF

A few days after our return to Hokianga we received intelligence that A Rowa, the father of Mooetara, and the eldest chief in the district, was dead. These deaths, when they occur among men of rank, are generally accompanied by some horrible scenes of butchery among their slaves—a common custom among all savages, but practised here (I was informed) with peculiar cruelty. We went on shore to witness the ceremony of A Rowa's lying in state, hoping at the same time that our presence might induce them to dispense with some of those barbarous cruelties which generally accompany their funeral rites. We had, indeed, every reason to think we had conjectured rightly, for nothing of the kind took place; which was considered by all as a circumstance somewhat remarkable. A great concourse of savages had assembled all round the village of the deceased chief, and there was a tremendous firing of muskets, but no particular marks of grief. I spoke to Mooetara, and requested, as a favour, if it were not breaking through their established rules, that he would conduct me to the body of his father. He accordingly led me to the outside of the village; and under a rude hut (constructed for the purpose) lay the body of the deceased chief, closely covered up with mats, leaving only part of the face and head exposed; in his hair was stuck a profusion of long white feathers, by way of ornament. Two women (whom I understood were his wives) sat close to the corpse; they were painted all over with red ochre, and seemed to perform the parts of chief mourners. These kept up a low moaning noise, and occasionally whisked off the flies from the face of the deceased. The women, the corpse, the hut, and the ground for some space round them, were all strictly tapued. Some bundles of fish, and some calabashes filled with oil, were left close by the body, intended for his consumption during his passage to the next world.

I imagine that one reason of no outrage having been committed during this solemn occasion was our brig being on the point of sailing, and previous to her departure a great deal of traffic was expected to be carried on with the natives, for there was still a considerable quantity of muskets undisposed of; and I think, in this instance, avarice overcame filial affection—the minds of the chief's family being so intent upon obtaining good bargains, that they had not time to sit and mourn over their departed parent, nor to work themselves up into a paroxysm of passion sufficiently violent to cause them to murder their slaves. This afforded me a convincing proof that as soon as they are occupied by commerce, or the useful arts, their barbarous rites will gradually be discontinued, and will speedily cease altogether.

Our brig having sailed, we were again alone with these wild yet interesting people. We expected our stay might be about six months, and had provided a stock-in-trade, consisting of a barrel of powder, half a dozen muskets, some fish-hooks, and a quantity of tobacco. Everything we possessed we delivered into the hands of the natives, who accounted to us for the stock thus entrusted to their management with the most scrupulous exactness. Nothing can be fairer than their mode of bartering with the Europeans; the prices are fixed; ten large hogs, or 120 baskets of potatoes (about a ton and a-half), are given for a musket; for small articles, such as fish, Indian corn, or fruits, the ready money are fish-hooks and tobacco. As we were now about to become inhabitants of New Zealand, it became necessary that we should be well acquainted with the particulars of their methods of "doing business," and that we should apply ourselves diligently to the study of the language, which we acquired much more readily than I had anticipated.

CHAPTER XXII

BRUTAL MURDER OF A WIFE

A few days after the departure of the brig I witnessed a specimen of their summary method of executing justice. A chief, resident in the village, had proof of the infidelity of one of his wives; and, being perfectly sure of her guilt, he took his patoo-patoo (or stone hatchet) and proceeded to his hut, where this wretched woman was employed in household affairs. Without mentioning the cause of his suspicion, or once upbraiding her, he deliberately aimed a blow at her head, which killed her on the spot; and, as she was a slave, he dragged the body to the outside of the village, and there left it to be devoured by the dogs. The account of this transaction was soon brought to us, and we proceeded to the place to request permission to bury the body of the murdered woman, which was immediately granted. Accordingly, we procured a couple of slaves, who assisted us to carry the corpse down to the beach, where we interred it in the most decent manner we could.

This was the second murder I was very nearly a witness to since my arrival; and the indifference with which each had been spoken of induced me to believe that such barbarities were events of frequent occurrence; yet the manners of all seemed kind and gentle towards each other; but infidelity in a wife is never forgiven here; and, in general, if the lover can be taken, he also is sacrificed along with the adulteress. Truth obliges me to confess that, notwithstanding these horrors staring them in the face, they will, if opportunity offers, indulge in an intrigue.

CHAPTER XXIII

ANOTHER JOURNEY TO BAY OF ISLANDS

As there were two roads across to the Bay of Islands, and I was anxious to see as much of the country as possible, I determined that my second journey should be by the longest route. I set off, accompanied only by a native boy to carry a small portmanteau and to serve me as a guide. As, on my former journey, we travelled many miles through thick tangled forests, fatiguing beyond description. In the midst of our toilsome progress, night frequently overtook us; then, by means of my fowling-piece, I procured a light, the boy made a fire, and we passed the night in this vast wilderness, far from the habitation of any human being! At daybreak we resumed our journey, and at length (about ten o'clock) we emerged from the wood, and entered upon extensive plains. These were not naked deserts, similar to the ones I had passed through on my former route, but were diversified with bush and brake, with a number of small villages scattered in various directions. At mid-day we arrived at what in New Zealand is considered a town of great size and importance, called Ty-a-my. It is situated on the sides of a beautiful hill, the top surmounted by a pa, in the midst of a lonely and extensive plain, covered with plantations of Indian corn, Kumara and potatoes. This is the principal inland settlement, and, in point of quiet beauty and fertility, it equalled any place I had ever seen in the various countries I have visited. Its situation brought forcibly to my remembrance the scenery around Canterbury.

We found the village totally deserted, all the inhabitants being employed in their various plantations; they shouted to us as we passed, thus bidding us welcome, but did not leave their occupations to receive us. To view the cultivated parts of this country from an eminence a person might easily imagine himself in a civilised land; for miles around the village of Ty-a-my nothing but beautiful green fields present themselves to the eye. The exact rows in which they plant their Indian corn would do credit to a first-rate English farmer, and the way in which they prepare the soil is admirable. The greatest deficiency which I observed in the country around me was the total absence of fences; and this defect occasions the natives a great deal of trouble, which might very easily be avoided. Hogs are the principal part of their wealth, with which, at all times, they can traffic with vessels touching at their ports. These animals, consequently, are of the utmost importance to them; but during the growth of their crops, the constant watching the hogs require to keep them out of the plantations consumes more time than would effectually fence in their whole country; but I have no doubt, as they already begin to follow our advice and adopt our plans, they will soon see the utility of fencing in their land. I have at various times held many conversations with different chiefs on this subject, all of whom have acknowledged the propriety of so doing.

A few miles after leaving this beautiful village we came to a spot covered with heaps of cinders and hillocks of volcanic matter. I found all these hillocks small craters, but none of them, burning; and for miles our road lay through ashes and lava. These fires must have been extinguished many ages since, as there is not the slightest tradition among any of the natives of their ever having been burning.

After passing over this lava, our journey lay through a very swampy country, intersected with streams. I got completely wearied with stripping to wade through them, so that at length I plunged in clothes and all. At the close of a most fatiguing day's march, we arrived in sight of the bay, having travelled over an extent of about fifty miles since the morning! No canoe being in sight, and we being too distant to make signals to our brig, we had to pass another night in bivouac on a part of the beach called Waitangi; and as it did not rain we slept pretty comfortably. The next morning I procured a canoe, and went on board our vessel.

The day following the brig took her final departure from New Zealand, and we bade farewell to Captain Kent. We now formally placed ourselves under the protection of King George, who seemed highly pleased with his charge; and in a few days three good houses were ready for our reception—one for ourselves, a second for our stores, and a third for our servants. But our pleasant prospects were soon obscured by a circumstance totally unexpected, which placed us in a most critical situation, and which we had every reason to fear would lead to our total destruction.

CHAPTER XXIV

VISIT OF A WAR PARTY

I was roused one morning at daybreak by my servant running in with the intelligence that a great number of war canoes were crossing the bay. As King George had told us but the evening before that he expected a visit from Ta-ri-ah, a chief of the tribe called Ngapuhis, whose territory lay on the opposite side of the bay, and given us to understand that Ta-ri-ah was a man not to be trusted, and therefore feared some mischief might happen if he really came, the sight of these war canoes naturally caused us considerable alarm, and we sincerely wished that the visit was over.

We dressed ourselves with the utmost expedition, and walked down to the beach. The landing of these warriors was conducted with a considerable degree of order, and could I have divested myself of all ideas of danger I should have admired the sight excessively. All our New Zealand friends—the tribe of Shulitea—were stripped naked, their bodies were oiled, and all were completely armed; their muskets were loaded, their cartouch boxes were fastened round their waists, and their patoo-patoos were fixed to their wrists. Their hair was tied up in a tight knot at the top of their heads, beautifully ornamented with feathers of the albatross. As the opposite party landed, ours all crouched on the ground, their eyes fixed on their visitors, and perfectly silent. When the debarkation was completed I observed the chief, Ta-ri-ah, put himself at their head, and march towards us with his party formed closely and compactly, and armed with muskets and paddles. When they came very near they suddenly stopped. Our party continued still mute, with their firelocks poised ready for use. For the space of a few minutes all was still, each party glaring fiercely on the other; and they certainly formed one of the most beautiful and extraordinary pictures I had ever beheld. The foreground was formed by a line of naked savages, each resting on one knee, with musket advanced, their gaze fixed on the opposite party, their fine, broad, muscular backs contrasting with the dark foliage in front, and catching the gleam of the rising sun. The strangers were clothed in the most grotesque manner imaginable—some armed, some naked, some with long beards, others were painted all over with red ochre; every part of each figure was quite still, except the rolling and glaring of their eyes on their opponents. The background was formed by the beach, and a number of their beautiful war canoes dancing on the waves; while, in the distance, the mountains on the opposite side of the bay were just tinged with the varied and beautiful colours of the sun, then rising in splendour from behind them.

The stillness of this extraordinary scene did not last long. The Ngapuhis commenced a noisy and discordant song and dance, yelling, jumping, and making the most hideous faces. This was soon answered by a loud shout from our party, who endeavoured to outdo the Ngapuhis in making horrible distortions of their countenances; then succeeded another dance from our visitors, after which our friends made a rush, and in a sort of rough joke set them running. Then all joined in a pell-mell sort of encounter, in which numerous hard blows were given and received; then all the party fired their pieces in the air, and the ceremony of landing was thus deemed completed. They then approached each other, and began rubbing noses; and those who were particular friends cried and lamented over each other.

The slaves now commenced the labour of making fires to cook the morning meal, while the chiefs, squatting down, formed a ring, or, rather, an oblong circle, on the ground; then one at a time rose up, and made long speeches, which they did in a manner peculiar to themselves. The speaker, during his harangue, keeps running backwards and forwards within the oblong space, using the most violent but appropriate gesticulation; so expressive, indeed, of the subject on which he is speaking, that a spectator who does not understand their language can form a tolerable idea as to what the affair is then under debate. The orator is never interrupted in his speech; but, when he finishes and sits down, another immediately rises up and takes his place, so that all who choose have an opportunity of delivering their sentiments, after which the assembly breaks up.

Though the meeting of these hostile tribes had thus ended more amicably than King George and his party could have expected, it was easily to be perceived that the Ngapuhis were determined on executing some atrocity or depredations before their return; they accordingly pretended to recollect some old offence committed by the English settlers at the other end of the beach. They proceeded thither, and first attacked and broke open the house of a blacksmith, and carried off every article it contained. They then marched to the residence of an English captain (who was in England), and plundered it of everything that could be taken away, and afterwards sent word they intended to return to our end of the beach. Our fears were greatly increased by finding that our friends were not sufficiently strong to protect us from the superior force of the Ngapuhis, and our chief, George, being himself (we supposed) conscious of his inability, had left us to depend upon our own resources.

CHAPTER XXV

BURNED OUT OF HOUSE AND HOME

We now called a council of war of all the Europeans settled here; and it was unanimously resolved that we should protect and defend our houses and property, and fortify our position in the best way we could. Captain Duke had in his possession four twelve-pounders, and these we brought in front of the enclosure in which our huts were situated, and were all entirely employed in loading them with round and grape shot, and had made them all ready for action, when, to our consternation and dismay, we found we had a new and totally unexpected enemy to contend with. By some accident one of our houses was in flames. Our situation was now perilous in the extreme. The buildings, the work of English carpenters, were constructed of dry rushes and well-seasoned wood, and this was one of a very respectable size, and we had hoped, in a very few days, would be finished fit for our removing into.

For some seconds we stood in mute amazement, not knowing to which point to direct our energies. As the cry of "fire" was raised, groups of natives came rushing from all directions upon our devoted settlement, stripping off their clothes, and yelling in the most discordant pitch of voice. I entered the house, and brought out one of my trunks, but on attempting to return a second time I found it filled with naked savages, tearing everything to pieces, and carrying away whatever they could lay their hands upon. The fierce raging of the flames, the heat from the fire, the yells of the men, and the shrill cries of the women, formed, altogether, a horrible combination; added to all this was the mortification of seeing all our property carried off in different directions, without the least possibility of our preventing it. The tribe of the Ngapuhis (who, when the fire began, were at the other end of the beach) left their operations in that quarter and poured down upon us to share in the general plunder. Never shall I forget the countenance of the chief, as he rushed forward at the head of his destroying crew! He was called "The Giant," and he was well worthy of the name, being the tallest and largest man I had ever seen; he had an immense bushy black beard, and grinned exultingly when he saw the work of destruction proceeding with such rapidity, and kept shouting loudly to his party to excite them to carry off all they could.

A cask containing seventy gallons of rum now caught fire and blew up with a terrible explosion; and, the wind freshening considerably, huge volumes of smoke and flame burst out in every direction. Two of our houses were so completely enveloped that we had given up all hopes of saving them. The third, which was a beautifully carved tapued one, some little distance from the others, and which we had converted into a store and magazine, was now the only object of our solicitude and terror. For, besides the valuable property of various kinds which were deposited within it, it contained several barrels of gunpowder! It was in vain we attempted to warn the frantic natives to retire from the vicinity of this danger. At length we persuaded about a dozen of the most rational to listen while we explained to them the cause of our alarm; and they immediately ascended to the roof, where, with the utmost intrepidity and coolness, they kept pouring water over the thatch, thus lessening the probability of an immediate explosion. About this time we noticed the reappearance of King George, which circumstance rekindled our hopes. He was armed with a thick stick, which he laid heavily on the backs of such of his subjects as were running away with our property, thus forcing them to relinquish their prizes, and to lay them down before his own mansion, where all was safe. By this means a great deal was recollected. The fire was now nearly extinguished; but our two really tolerably good houses were reduced to a heap of smoking ruins, and the greater part of what belonged to us was taken away by the Ngapuhis.

This calamity had made us acquainted with another of their barbarous customs, which is, whenever a misfortune happens to a community, or an individual, every person, even the friends of his own tribe, fall upon and strip him of all he has remaining. As an unfortunate fish, when struck by a harpoon, is instantly surrounded and devoured by his companions, so in New Zealand, when a chief is killed, his former friends plunder his widow and children; and they, in revenge, ill-use and even murder their slaves—thus one misfortune gives birth to various cruelties. During the fire, our allies proved themselves the most adroit and active thieves imaginable, though previously to that event we had never lost an article, although everything we possessed was open to them.

When we questioned them about our property, they frankly told us where it was; and, after some difficulty in settling the amount of its ransom, we got most of our things back again, with the exception of such as had been carried off by the Ngapuhis.

Upon the cruelty of this custom I shall make no comments. Probably I should have remained in ignorance of this savage law, had I not had the misfortune to become its victim.

By redeeming from the natives what they had purloined from the fire, we had restored to us some of our boxes, desks, and clothes; but all our little comforts towards housekeeping were irretrievably lost. When the fire was over we received a visit from one of the missionaries, who made us a cold offer of assistance. We accepted a little tea, sugar and some few articles of crockery from them; but, although they knew we stood there houseless, amongst a horde of savages, they never offered us the shelter of their roofs. I am very sure that had the calamity befallen them, we should immediately have offered our huts, and shared with them everything we possessed. Here was an opportunity of practically showing the "pagans" (as they termed the New Zealanders) the great Christian doctrine of "doing to others as we would they should do unto us." I must acknowledge I was sometimes mortified at being obliged to sleep (three of us huddled up close together) in a small New Zealand hut, filled with filth and vermin of all kinds, while at only two miles' distance from us stood a neat village, abounding in every comfort that a bountiful British public could provide; and we, members of that community, and, indeed, partly contributors to the funds for its support.

The high state of excitement into which the savages had been thrown by the late conflagration gradually subsided, and as we had escaped the dreaded calamity of our magazine blowing up, we began to look with calmness on our desolate condition, and draw comfort from thinking how much worse we might have been circumstanced than we then were. I hope our distress may prove a benefit to future sojourners in this country, by showing them the great importance of forming a proper magazine for powder. The agonies I suffered in contemplating the destruction which six barrels of powder, each of an hundredweight, would cause amongst a mob of several hundred naked savages, it is impossible to imagine!

King George, as well as all his people, were most anxious to build us a new habitation entirely themselves. They requested us to give them the dimensions of the various dwellings, and said we should have no further trouble about them. A party accordingly proceeded to the bush to collect materials. They first formed the skeleton of a cottage containing three rooms, with slight sticks, firmly tied together with strips of flax. While this was in progress, another party was collecting rushes (which grow plentifully in the neighbourhood, called Ra-poo). These they spread in the sun for twenty-four hours, when they considered them sufficiently dry. They then thatched every part of the house, which for neatness and strength was equal to anything I had ever seen. The doors and windows we employed our carpenter to make, these being luxuries quite beyond the comprehension of the natives. We were thus tolerably well lodged again; and our time passed on tranquilly, almost every day developing some fresh trait of character amongst these children of nature.

CHAPTER XXVI

A HOSTILE DEMONSTRATION

I went to reside for a short time at a village about half a mile distant, where there was a pretty good house vacant. It was called Ma-to-we, and belonged to a chief named Atoi, a relation of George's, but a much younger man. His power was not so great, and he was every way subject to the authority of the tribe under whose protection I had placed myself. One morning, at daybreak, we were roused by the hasty approach of King George and all his warriors towards Ma-to-we. All were fully equipped for war, and each countenance looked fierce and wild. Our late misfortunes having rendered us more than usually anxious, this hostile appearance gave us considerable alarm. We left our house to inquire the reason thereof, and saw George and his followers enter the village, pull down several fences, fire a few muskets in the air, dance a most hideous dance of defiance, and then depart; but not one word of explanation could we obtain from him. In the course of the morning, however, the women acquainted us with the cause of this mysterious proceeding, which determined me to remove my things back again to George's village of Kororarika as soon as possible.

The affair was simply this: Atoi had two wives. During the time of our visit to his village, he was absent, and had entrusted these women to the care of his brother; but he, instead of being faithful to the trust reposed in him, had actually seduced one of them. This circumstance came to the knowledge of George, and he, feeling for the honour of his absent friend, immediately proceeded to the village, and thus gave the parties warning that he was fully aware of the nature of their proceedings. He had also dispatched a messenger to Atoi, to inform him of his disgrace, and to request his immediate return. In the course of the day it was expected he would arrive, and bring with him a strong party of friends, all burning with revenge, and eager to punish his brother for his unnatural perfidy. It was thought that unless George interfered, much bloodshed might ensue;

and it may readily be imagined how anxious we were that this dreaded meeting should be over; yet I (for one) had determined that I would be a witness of it. Therefore, when word was brought to me that Atoi was crossing the bay, I hastened down to the beach. There I found all parties assembled from both villages. George and his followers, who were to act as mediators, sat immediately in front of the place of landing; behind them were Atoi's brother and all his partizans; and in the rear were all the women and children, with about a dozen white faces scattered amongst them. The scene was picturesque and exceedingly interesting. It was near the close of a lovely summer's day—the sun, fast sinking towards the horizon, threw a warm and mellow glow over the wide expanse of the far-spreading bay, whose smooth waters were only disturbed by the approaching canoe cutting its foamy way. It was crowded with naked warriors, urging their rapid course towards the shore; and we heard the loud and furious song of the chief, animating his friends to exertion; we saw his frantic gestures, as he stood in the centre of his canoe, brandishing his weapons. As they came near the place of landing, George ran into the stream, and as the canoe touched the shore, attacked Atoi, but in a playful manner, splashing water over him. Thus irritated, Atoi jumped on land, and, with a double-barrelled musket in his hand, ran towards his brother, and doubtless would have killed him on the spot, had he not been prevented. I now saw the advantage of George and his party being present. He and three of his subjects seized upon Atoi, and tried to wrest the weapon from his hands, which if they had been able to effect, a mortal combat could not take place, such being the custom here. Atoi was a very powerful man of about thirty, and those who attacked him had a most difficult task; twice he broke from them; and I then watched the countenance of his brother, which was perfectly cool and collected, though the firelock was in readiness, and the finger on the trigger, which might despatch him instantly. All parties sat perfectly quiet during the desperate struggle; one of the barrels of Atoi's piece went off, and the contents flew amongst us, without, however, doing any material injury; and, finally, the musket was wrested out of his hands. He then sat still for about twenty minutes, to recover his breath, when he seized a club and rushed upon his brother (for mortal weapons were now prohibited). The brother started up, armed in the same manner; some heavy blows passed between them; when, having thrown aside their clubs, they grappled each other firmly, and a dreadful struggle ensued. As they were both completely naked, their hair was the only thing to take hold by; but being long, thick, and strong, it afforded a firm grasp, and they committed desperate havoc on each other's persons. At this period of the fight their poor old mother, who was quite blind, came forward to try and separate the combatants; the sister and younger brothers now followed her example; and, finally, the fair and frail cause of all this commotion.

The brothers, having completely exhausted their strength, were easily separated; and as their friends had carefully removed all weapons out of their reach, they of course were deprived of the means of injuring each other. The members of Atoi's family, together with a few friends, now sat down in a circle, to converse and consult on the affair. Atoi's wife totally denied the charge, and protested her innocence, and many circumstances were brought forward to corroborate her statements. The husband at length was satisfied, and all parties were reconciled.

CHAPTER XXVII

THE LAW OF RETALIATION

This affair was scarcely terminated, when we found that another of a still more serious nature was likely to arise from it and would threaten the peace of both villages. When King George sent his messenger to inform Atoi of the infidelity of his wife, the infuriated husband assaulted the man, and it was rumoured that he had killed him. This was an offence not to be forgiven, and George was so exasperated by it that he vowed he would exterminate the whole of Atoi's tribe. A native, however, arrived with the intelligence that the man was not dead, but only wounded. This did not seem to allay George's feelings of resentment, and he instantly made great preparations for war. When our anxiety was wound up to the utmost, we were greatly astonished to see Atoi and all his friends approach our settlement, totally unarmed. George went out to meet them, looking so full of rage that I thought Atoi stood but a slight chance for his life. After a great deal of violent pantomimic action and grimace, the apology offered by Atoi was accepted, and the visit was concluded by a grand war-dance and sham fight performed in their best manner. King George, in the fulness of his heart at this complete restoration of friendship, gave a great feast of kumaras and fish, to which we added some tobacco; and the whole of the party seated themselves by each other with the utmost sociality—a convincing proof that animosity is not long an inmate of their breasts.

I took every opportunity of inquiring into the nature of their laws and mode of government, and I found that, in general, their method of redressing wrongs was very summary, and that their ideas of what was strictly just were, for the most part, simple and equitable. For any theft, or offence of that sort, committed by one tribe on another, the parties are called to instant account. If one native takes from another any part of his possessions, the party injured has a right to retaliate, and the party retaliated upon must not make the slightest resistance. We ourselves experienced a proof of this. Some part of our property, which we supposed had been destroyed by our late fire, we had been told was to be found in the hut of a neighbouring chief. We one day took advantage of his absence, searched the hut ourselves, and discovered our things carefully deposited therein. Thus assured of the fact, we laid our complaint before King George, who, after hearing our story to the end, replied, "Well, my friends, you must go to the hut and take away all your property, and whatever else you may find, which you may think sufficient payment for the injury you have received." We accordingly proceeded to the chief's dwelling, whom we found standing at his door. We charged him with having robbed us, and entered the house to seize our property. He held down his head, and seemed ashamed and overpowered at this discovery. He did not attempt to vindicate his conduct, but quietly allowed us not only to take away all that had belonged to us, but likewise a musket and double-barrelled gun, which he concluded he had lost for ever. These we had only taken away temporarily to deter him from theft in future, for a few days after we brought them back to him, to his infinite delight and astonishment.

I was frequently shocked during my residence in this country by the number of accidents which continually happened to the natives from gunpowder, and not even the saddest experience could render them more careful. We were doubtful of the strength of a French fowling-piece we had, so we loaded it to the muzzle and discharged it, in order to prove it. Some young chiefs, who saw us do this (approving of this method), as soon as they returned home loaded a musket in the same manner, and then discharged it; but not managing the affair as we did—by means of a string fastened to the trigger—the piece burst, and mangled two of them dreadfully, and we got greatly blamed for showing them what was considered so bad an example.

A few months since a native came from the interior driving a quantity of pigs to barter for powder; he obtained several pounds' weight, and set off to return home. On his journey he passed the night in a hut, and for safety put the bag of powder under his head as a pillow; and as a New Zealander always sleeps with a fire close to him, the consequence was, in the course of the night the fire communicated to the powder, and destroyed the man and the whole of his family, who were journeying with him.

CHAPTER XXVIII

A WAR EXPEDITION AND A CANNIBAL FEAST

Last year a chief, and cousin of King George, named Pomare, was defeated and killed by the people of the Thames, and George was now resolved to revenge his death. This determination having become known, we had a constant succession of visitors, and a considerable number of blows, scratches, and rubbing noses were the consequence. Our beach presented a most interesting and busy scene. A dozen superb war canoes were lying ready to convey the forces; and, considering their limited means, the solidity of their structure and the carved work on them are surprising. None but men of rank are allowed to work upon them, and they labour like slaves. Some canoes were to be lengthened; others patched; others were condemned to be broken up, and the fragments taken to complete the new ones. Every morning we were awakened by the sound of the hammer and saw, and they were much gratified by our walking down to their dockyard to observe the progress they made, and by giving our opinions of their work. They thankfully received any hint we gave them as to better methods of completing or proceeding with their operations. Here were carvers, painters, caulkers, and sailmakers, all working in their different departments with great good humour and industry. Some of their vessels were eighty feet long, and were entirely covered with beautiful carving. Their form was light and delicate, and if their intentions were hostile towards us, they would be very formidable alongside any merchant man. If our Government should determine to colonise any part of New Zealand, they would find the natives hardy and willing assistants, and very different from the natives of New South Wales.

Maori War Expedition (With Mission boat accompanying it.)

As their canoes were ready for launching, they ran them off the beach, jumped into them, and scudded across the bay with an almost incredible swiftness. When it is considered that in each canoe were seated eighty stout young men, each with a large paddle in his hand propelling the vessel forward, the velocity with which she flew may be imagined! It was in the midst of scenes like these that we were passing our time, and I had just become delighted with the appearance of innocence and industry so continually displayed by these people, when I was called upon to witness a sight which exhibited their character in its worst light, and confirmed all my horrible suspicions regarding their alleged cannibalism.

The New Zealanders have been long charged with cannibalism; but as no person of importance or celebrity had actually been a witness to the disgusting act, in pity to our nature such relations have been universally rejected, and much has been written to prove the non-existence of so hideous a propensity. It was my lot to behold it in all its horrors!

One morning, about eleven o'clock, after I had just returned from a long walk, Captain Duke informed me he had heard, from very good authority (though the natives wished it to be kept a profound secret), that in the adjoining village a female slave, named Matowe, had been put to death, and that the people were at that very time preparing her flesh for cooking. At the same time he reminded me of a circumstance which had taken place the evening before. Atoi had been paying us a visit, and, when going away, he recognised a girl whom he said was a slave that had run away from him; he immediately seized hold of her, and gave her in charge to some of his people. The girl had been employed in carrying wood for us; Atoi's laying claim to her had caused us no alarm for her life, and we had thought no more on the subject; but now, to my surprise and horror, I heard this poor girl was the victim they were preparing for the oven! Captain Duke and myself were resolved to witness this dreadful scene. We therefore kept our information as secret as possible, well knowing that if we had manifested our wishes they would have denied the whole affair. We set out, taking a circuitous route towards the village, and, being well acquainted with the road, we came upon them suddenly, and found them in the midst of their abominable ceremonies.

On a spot of rising ground, just outside the village, we saw a man preparing a native oven, which is done in the following simple manner:—A hole is made in the ground, and hot stones are put within it, and then all is covered up close. As we approached, we saw evident signs of the murder which had been perpetrated; bloody mats were strewed around, and a boy was standing by them actually laughing: he put his finger to his head, and then pointed towards a bush. I approached the bush, and there discovered a human head. My feelings of horror may be imagined as I recognised the features of the unfortunate girl I had seen forced from our village the preceding evening!

We ran towards the fire, and there stood a man occupied in a way few would wish to see. He was preparing the four-quarters of a human body for a feast; the large bones, having been taken out, were thrown aside, and the flesh being compressed, he was in the act of forcing it into the oven. While we stood transfixed by this terrible sight, a large dog, which lay before the fire, rose up, seized the bloody head, and walked off with it into the bushes, no doubt to hide it there for another meal! The man completed his task with the most perfect composure, telling us, at the same time, that the repast would not be ready for some hours!

Here stood Captain Duke and myself, both witnesses of a scene which many travellers have related, and their relations have invariably been treated with contempt; indeed, the veracity of those who had the temerity to relate such incredible events has been everywhere questioned. In this instance it was no warrior's flesh to be eaten; there was no enemy's blood to drink, in order to infuriate them. They had no revenge to gratify; no plea could they make of their passions having been roused by battle, nor the excuse that they eat their enemies to perfect their triumph. This was an action of unjustifiable cannibalism. Atoi, the chief, who had given orders for this cruel feast, had only the night before sold us four pigs for a few pounds of powder; so he had not even the excuse of want of food. After Captain Duke and myself had consulted with each other, we walked into the village, determining to charge Atoi with his brutality.

Atoi received us in his usual manner; and his handsome, open countenance could not be imagined to belong to so savage a monster as he had proved himself to be. I shuddered at beholding the unusual quantity of potatoes his slaves were preparing to eat with this infernal banquet. We talked coolly with him on the subject, for, as we could not prevent what had taken place, we were resolved to learn, if possible, the whole particulars. Atoi at first tried to make us believe he knew nothing about it, and that it was only a meal for his slaves; but we had ascertained it was for himself and his favourite companions. After various endeavours to conceal the fact, Atoi frankly owned that he was only waiting till the cooking was completed to partake of it. He added that, knowing the horror we Europeans held these feasts in, the natives were always most anxious to conceal them from us, and he was very angry that it had come to our knowledge; but, as he had acknowledged the fact, he had no objection to talk about it. He told us that human flesh required a greater number of hours to cook than any other; that if not done enough it was very tough, but when sufficiently cooked it was as tender as paper. He held in his hand a piece of paper, which he tore in illustration of his remark. He said the flesh then preparing would not be ready till next morning; but one of his sisters whispered in my ear that her brother was deceiving us, as they intended feasting at sunset.

We inquired why and how he had murdered the poor girl. He replied that running away from him to her own relations was her only crime. He then took us outside his village, and showed us the post to which she had been tied, and laughed to think how he had cheated her: "For," said he, "I told her I only intended to give her a flogging; but I fired, and shot her through the heart!" My blood ran cold at this relation, and I looked with feelings of horror at the savage while he related it. Shall I be credited when I again affirm that he was not only a handsome young man, but mild and genteel in his demeanour? He was a man we had admitted to our table, and was a general favourite with us all; and the poor victim to his bloody cruelty was a pretty girl of about sixteen years of age!

While listening to this frightful detail, we felt sick almost to fainting. We left Atoi, and again strolled towards the spot where this disgusting mess was cooking. Not a native was now near it: a hot, fetid steam kept occasionally bursting from the smothered mass; and the same dog we had seen with the head now crept from beneath the bushes, and sneaked towards the village. To add to the gloominess of the whole, a large hawk rose heavily from the very spot where the poor victim had been cut in pieces. My friend and I sat gazing on this melancholy place; it was a lowering, gusty day, and the moaning of the wind through the bushes, as it swept round the hill on which we were, seemed in unison with our feelings.

After some time spent in contemplating the miserable scene before us, during which we gave full vent to the most passionate exclamations of disgust, we determined to spoil this intended feast. This resolution formed, we rose to execute it. I ran off to our beach, leaving Duke on guard, and, collecting all the white men I could, I informed them of what had happened, and asked them if they would assist in destroying the oven and burying the remains of the girl. They consented, and each having provided himself with a shovel or a pickaxe, we repaired in a body to the spot. Atoi and his friends had by some means been informed of our intention, and they came out to prevent it. He used various threats to deter us, and seemed highly indignant; but as none of his followers appeared willing to come to blows, and seemed ashamed that such a transaction should have been discovered by us, we were permitted by them to do as we chose. We accordingly dug a tolerably deep grave; then we resolutely attacked the oven. On removing the earth and leaves, the shocking spectacle was presented to our view—the four quarters of a human body half roasted. During our work clouds of steam enveloped us, and the disgust created by our task was almost overpowering. We collected all the parts we could recognise; the heart was placed separately, we supposed, as a savoury morsel for the chief himself. We placed the whole in the grave, which we filled up as well as we could, and then broke and scattered the oven.

By this time the natives from both villages had assembled, and a scene similar to this was never before witnessed in New Zealand. Six unarmed men, quite unprotected (for there was not a single vessel in the harbour, nor had there been for a month), had attacked and destroyed all the preparations of the natives for what they consider a national feast; and this was done in the presence of a great body of armed chiefs, who had assembled to partake of it. After having finished this exploit, and our passion and disgust had somewhat subsided, I could not help feeling that we had acted very imprudently in thus tempting the fury of these savages, and interfering in an affair that certainly was no concern of ours; but as no harm accrued to any of our party, it plainly shows the influence "the white men" have already obtained over them; had the offence we committed been done by any hostile tribe, hundreds of lives would have been sacrificed.

The next day our old friend King George paid us a long visit, and we talked over the affair very calmly. He highly disapproved of our conduct. "In the first place," said he, "you did a foolish thing, which might have cost you your lives; and yet did not accomplish your purpose after all, as you merely succeeded in burying the flesh near the spot on which you found it. After you went away it was again taken up, and every bit was eaten"—a fact I afterwards ascertained by examining the grave and finding it empty. King George further said: "It was an old custom, which their fathers practised before them; and you had no right to interfere with their ceremonies. I myself," added he, "have left off eating human flesh, out of compliment to you white men; but you have no reason to expect the same compliance from all the other chiefs. What punishment have you in England for thieves and runaways?" We answered, "After trial, flogging or hanging." "Then," he replied, "the only difference in our laws is, you flog and hang, but we shoot and eat."

After thus reproving us, he became very communicative on the subject of cannibalism. He said, he recollected the time prior to pigs and potatoes being introduced into the island (an epoch of great importance to the New Zealanders), and stated that he was born and reared in an inland district, and the only food they then had consisted of fern roots and kumara; fish they never saw, and the only flesh he then partook of was human. But I will no longer dwell on this humiliating subject. Most white men who have visited the island have been sceptical on this point; I myself was before I had "ocular proof." Consequently I availed myself of the first opportunity to convince myself of the fact. I have reflected upon the subject, and am thoroughly satisfied that nothing will cure the natives of this dreadful propensity but the introduction of many varieties of animals, both wild and tame, and all would be sure to thrive in so mild and fine a climate.

CHAPTER XXIX

SLAVERY AMONG THE MAORIS

The scene I have just described brings into consideration the subject of slavery, as it now exists in New Zealand. That slavery should be the custom of savage nations and cannibals, is not a cause of wonder: they are the only class of human beings it ought to remain with. Here slavery assumes its most hideous shape! Every one they can effect a seizure of in an enemy's country becomes the slave of the captors. Chiefs are never made prisoners; they either fight to the last, or are killed on the spot, and their heads are preserved (by a peculiar method) as trophies. Children are greatly prized: these they bring to their dwellings, and they remain slaves for life. Upon the number of slaves a chief can muster he takes his rank as a man of wealth and consequence in society; and the only chance these wretched beings have of being released from their miseries, is their master getting into a rage, and murdering them without further ceremony.

On entering a village, a stranger instantly discovers which portion of its inhabitants are the slaves, though both the complexion and the dresses of all are alike. The free Zealander is a joyous, good-humoured looking man, full of laughter and vivacity, and is chattering incessantly; but the slaves have invariably a squalid, dejected look; they are never seen to smile, and appear literally half starved. The beauties characteristic of a New Zealander are his teeth and hair; the latter, in particular, is his pride and study; but the slaves have their heads half shorn. The male slave is not allowed to marry; and any intercourse with a female, if discovered, is generally punished by death. Never was there a body of men so completely cut off from all society as these poor slaves; they never can count, with certainty, on a single moment of life, as the savage caprice of their master may instantly deprive them of it. If, by chance, a slave should belong to a kind and good master, an accident happening to him, or any of his family, will probably prove equally fatal to the slave, as some are generally sacrificed on the death of a chief.

Thus these poor slaves are deprived of every hope and stimulus by which all other classes and individuals are animated; no good conduct of theirs towards their master, no attachment to his person or family, no fidelity or long service can ensure kind treatment. If the slave effect his escape to his own part of the country, he is there treated with contempt; and when he dies (if a natural death), his body is dragged to the outside of the village, there to be made sport of by the children, or to furnish food for the dogs! but more frequently his fate is to receive a fatal blow in a fit of passion, and then be devoured by his brutal master! Even the female slaves who, if pretty, are frequently taken as wives by their conquerors, have not a much greater chance of happiness, all being dependent upon the caprice of their owners.

When I can relate anything favourable to the missionaries, I invariably intend to do so, which will account for the introduction of the following: A few days since, I paid a visit to one of their settlements, and noticed a remarkably fine native woman attending as a servant. She was respectably dressed, and in every respect (except complexion) she was similar to a European. She spoke English fluently. Upon expressing my admiration of her, I was informed that this woman had been a slave of Hongi's, and that about a year previous he had lost one of his sons, and had determined to sacrifice this poor girl as an atonement. She was actually bound for the purpose, and nothing but the strong interference of the whole of the missionary society here could have saved her life. They exerted themselves greatly, and preserved her; and she had proved a faithful and valuable servant.

CHAPTER XXX

PIRATICAL SEIZURE OF A VESSEL

Before finally quitting the subject of slavery, I must give an account of some white men I saw in this state of degradation, and who belonged to a chief who visited us some weeks since. In the beginning of 1827, the Government of New South Wales hired the brig Wellington to convey a number of prisoners to Norfolk Island, most of whom were felons of the worst description: the greater part were under sentence of banishment for life. These desperadoes amounted to seventy-four; by far too many for the size of the brig, as those whose duty is was to guard them, and the crew of the vessel, were too few to keep them under subjection. When within a few days' sail of their destination, they rose on the guard, and, after a desperate struggle, made themselves masters of the vessel, which was a very fine one, and was well provided with arms and stores of every kind, amounting to a sufficiency to carry them to any part of the world they chose. But the machinations of the wicked rarely prosper, and this was another proof of the truth of the observation; for, after a stormy and violent debate among themselves, they at length determined to run for the Bay of Islands, and if any vessel more eligible was there, they were to take possession of her, and leave the Wellington behind, she having no register. It is but justice to them to state that they behaved with humanity to their captives, and no lives were lost: they appointed officers amongst themselves, and, with the assistance of the deposed captain, made this port. On their arrival here, they found two English whalers, the Sisters, Captain Duke, and the Harriet. The commanders, as is usual on these occasions, went immediately on board the newcomer. Captain Duke well knew the vessel, having seen her at Sydney; but, of course, had no idea of what had happened. The pirates received them with great civility, and deceived them with a false description of their voyage — of being bound to a southern port with prisoners; and the two captains, not having the slightest suspicion of who their hosts really were, passed a very merry evening with these marauders.

Soon, however, their bad management of the vessel, their want of discipline, and the general confusion on board, roused a vague suspicion in the minds of the two captains that all was not "quite right" on board the Wellington. The real captain, too, had succeeded in conveying a note to Duke, informing him of his situation, and claiming his assistance to recapture the brig, and entreating him to release them all from captivity.

This communication produced universal alarm, as both the whalers were quite unprovided for attack or defence, and all the missionary settlements lay quite at the mercy of this band of pirates. Had the latter acted with promptness and spirit, they might easily have made themselves masters of the whole; but while they were arguing and hesitating where they would make their first attack, the whalers were actively employed in getting their great guns out of the hold, and in preparing their vessels for defence; so that, by the time the pirates came to the resolution to attack them, the whalers were in a good posture for resistance, and finally became the assailants. Aided by the prompt assistance of the natives, the whole of these outlaws were taken into custody, with the exception of six. The extreme interest the savages took in capturing these deluded men was truly astonishing. When they were made to understand that these were King George's (of England) slaves, who had broken loose, they knew, from their own laws, that they ought to be taken, and they displayed a great deal of courage and address in approaching and securing them.

The pirates (having many passengers and others in their power) stipulated that they should be landed at Kororarika, unmolested by any of the English. This was granted; but no sooner were they left by themselves than a party of natives came forward, seized and bound them, stripped off their clothes, and, after dressing themselves up in them, conducted their prisoners on board the whalers; but notwithstanding the anxiety of the whalers to secure the whole, and the activity of the natives, six of them found means to elude the search, and here they now are.

The day on which our houses were burned, these six landed in the train of one of the chiefs; and I have since entertained a suspicion that it was their desire of revenge that occasioned the destruction of our property at the time the calamity happened. I chanced to be in the house alone, and was amazed by seeing an Englishman enter the hut with his face tattooed all over. Not being aware he was one of the runaways from the Wellington, I spoke to him. He slunk into our cooking-house on pretence of lighting his pipe, and before ten minutes had elapsed, the house was in flames.

CHAPTER XXXI

THE CLIMATE AND PRODUCTIONS

The summer was now far advanced, and never, during its progress, had we been incommoded by any very hot weather. Our house was generally crowded with visitors: for, as it was the workmanship of King George and his people, they were prodigiously proud of it, and each seemed to think he had an undoubted right to sit in it as much as he liked. This, at times, we felt as a great annoyance; but we were obliged to be very cautious not to say or do anything that should give offence to them, as all were exceedingly irritable, and we felt it to be most essential to our comfort to continue on friendly terms with them.

Although we were situated in the same latitude as Sydney, we found the climate of New Zealand infinitely superior. Moderate heats and beautifully clear skies succeeded each other every day. We were quite free from those oppressive, feverish heats which invariably prevail in the middle of the day at Sydney, and from those hot pestilential winds which are the terror of the inhabitants of New South Wales; nor were we subject to those long droughts, which are often the ruin of the Australian farmer. The temperature here was neither too hot nor too cold, neither too wet nor too dry. Reflecting on this country—its situation, inhabitants, and climate—I felt convinced that, if it were the object of our Government to form a new colony, they could not select a more desirable spot than New Zealand. When we left Sydney, a disease was raging there of a most disagreeable nature, namely, catarrh. As usual, it affected strongly the eyes and nose, and generally proved fatal to the very old and to children. We found the poor natives here subject to the same complaint, which they called the "Murray," or "Murraybad"; and they declared they caught it from us Europeans.

I could scarcely refrain from laughing while witnessing the strange methods they adopted to effect a cure. Sometimes they would envelope their heads entirely in green leaves, at other times they would almost roast themselves in a heated hut; but their universal remedy, and the one they generally found successful, was starvation, which is, in fact, the doctor who cures them of all the diseases the Europeans have imported amongst them: and, I confess, I have often been amazed at their rapid recovery from maladies which I should have thought incurable. The other day I asked the opinion of a clever medical man, who came here with one of the whalers, and he informed me the only cases he had met with amongst the natives, which terminated fatally, were a few instances of consumption.

After the novelty of our savage life began to wear away, I rambled much about the country, in order to form some judgment of its capability of improvement. I never possessed any practical knowledge of farming, and therefore cannot give a scientific opinion or description of the different soils. In whatever direction I travelled, and at this time I had crossed the country in various directions several times, the soil appeared to me to be fat and rich, and also well watered. From every part of it which the natives have cultivated, the produce has been immense. Here, where the finest samples of the human race are to be found, the largest and finest timber grows, and every vegetable (yet planted) thrives, the introduction of European grasses, fruits, etc., etc., would be a great desideratum. Were this done, in a very short time farms would be more eagerly sought after here than they now are in New South Wales. All the fruits and plants hitherto introduced by the missionary establishments have succeeded wonderfully. Peaches and water melons now were in full season; the natives brought baskets full of them to our door every day, which they exchanged with us for the merest trifles, such as a fish-hook, or a button.

Indian corn was likewise very abundant, but as the natives did not possess any means or knowledge of grinding it, they were not aware of its full value. Their only method of cooking it was one very disgusting to Europeans. They soaked the ear in water till it was quite soft and sour, the smell from which was exceedingly offensive; they then placed it in their earth ovens to bake, and when they partook of it they seemed to enjoy it very much.

In one of my journeys across the island I was accompanied by my Scotch friend, Mr. Shand, who prided himself very much upon his general knowledge of agricultural pursuits; and when I indulged in some sudden bursts of admiration at the beauty of the surrounding prospect, he would invariably check my enthusiasm, by observing that no animals could possibly live in a country so overgrown with fern, and where no grass was indigenous. These observations, often repeated, obliged me to qualify my admiration of this picturesque and beautiful land; but my surprise, and I may say my triumph, were complete when, on approaching the missionary village of Kirikiri, we fell in with a herd of at least a hundred fat cattle, browsing on the sides of the hill, and having nothing else but this very fern to eat; and, on inquiry, we found they gave as good milk, and were in as healthy a condition, as when they grazed on the rich grasses of Lincolnshire.

My friend, Captain Duke, made great preparations for the return of his ships, and purchased many pigs to be salted. The self-denial of the natives is wonderful: though very fond of animal food, they sell the whole to us Europeans for the means of war; thus conquering the appetite for the purpose of possessing arms to make them terrible in the sight of their enemies. This feeling, properly directed, may lead to their becoming a great nation. In the course of our saltings and picklings of pork, owing to the warmth of the weather, a considerable quantity was spoiled. I recommended its being immediately thrown into the sea, but Duke, who knew the propensities of the people better than I did, and wished to ingratiate himself among them, sent for some of his favourites, and presented them with the damaged meat, with which they marched off highly delighted, and made a public feast of it in the evening.

New Zealand Method of Tattooing. (From a sketch by A. Earle.)

CHAPTER XXXII

THE ART OF TATTOOING

The art of tattooing has been brought to such perfection here, that whenever we have seen a New Zealander whose skin is thus ornamented, we have admired him. It is looked upon as answering the same purposes as clothes. When a chief throws off his mats, he seems as proud of displaying the beautiful ornaments figured on his skin as a first-rate exquisite is in exhibiting himself in his last fashionable attire. It is an essential part of war-like preparations. The whole of this district of Kororarika was preparing for the approaching war. Their canoes, muskets, powder and balls, increased daily; and a very ingenious artist, called Aranghie, arrived to carry on this important branch of his art, which was soon placed in requisition, for all the mighty men in the neighbourhood were one by one under his operating hands.

As this "professor" was a near neighbour of mine, I frequently paid him a visit in his "studio," and he returned the compliment whenever he had time to spare. He was considered by his countrymen a perfect master in the art of tattooing, and men of the highest rank and importance were in the habit of travelling long journeys in order to put their skins under his skilful hands. Indeed, so highly were his works esteemed, that I have seen many of his drawings exhibited even after death. A neighbour of mine very lately killed a chief who had been tattooed by Aranghie, and, appreciating the artist's work so highly, he skinned the chieftain's thighs, and covered his cartouch box with it.

I was astonished to see with what boldness and precision Aranghie drew his designs upon the skin, and what beautiful ornaments he produced; no rule and compasses could be more exact than the lines and circles he formed. So unrivalled is he in his profession, that a highly-finished face of a chief from the hands of this artist is as greatly prized in New Zealand as a head from the hands of Sir Thomas Lawrence is amongst us. It was most gratifying to behold the respect these savages pay to the fine arts. This "professor" was merely a *kooky* or slave, but by skill and industry he raised himself to an equality with the greatest men of his country; and as every chief who employed him always made him some handsome present, he soon became a man of wealth, and was constantly surrounded by such important personages as Pungho Pungho, Ruky Ruky, Kivy Kivy, Aranghy Tooker, etc., etc. My friend Shulitea (King George) sent him every day the choicest things from his own table. Though thus basking in the full sunshine of court favour, Aranghie, like a true genius, was not puffed up with pride by his success, for he condescended to come and take tea with me almost every evening. He was delighted with my drawings, particularly with a portrait I made of him. He copied so well, and seemed to enter with such interest into the few lessons of painting I gave him, that if I were returning from here direct to England, I would certainly bring him with me, as I look upon him as a great natural genius.

One of the important personages who came to the village to employ the talent of our artist was a *Mr.* Rooky Rooky (and he was always very particular in remembering the *Mister*); he brought four of his wives with him, leaving six more at home (polygamy in New Zealand being allowed to any extent). One of this man's wives was a little girl not more than ten years of age, and she excited a great deal of interest amongst us, which, when he discovered, he became very anxious to dispose of her to any of us. He importuned us incessantly on the subject, saying she was his slave, and offered her in exchange for a musket.

Specimens of Tattooed Faces and Thigh. (From "Expedition de l'Astrolabe.")

CHAPTER XXXIII

TRIBAL GOVERNMENT AND RELIGION

Though from my increased knowledge of the language, I was enabled to hold longer conversations, I could not discover that the New Zealanders had any universal form of government: there appeared to me to be no public bodies, or any functionaries employed by the people. Each chief seemed to possess absolute power over his own slaves, and there his authority terminated. Wealth made him feared by his foes, but gave him no influence over his friends. All offence offered to any one of a tribe (or clan) is instantly followed by some act of retaliation by the aggrieved party; and if one tribe is too weak to contend against the one from whom they have received the injury, they call in the aid of another. But should the offence be of a very aggravated nature, and several families be injured by it, a meeting of the chiefs is called. They assemble in one of their forts, and, after a discussion, decide either for an amicable adjustment, or for an exterminating war. Thus these misguided beings are continually destroying each other for some imaginary insult.

I became acquainted with a few venerable men of truly noble and praiseworthy characters, such as would do honour to any age, country, or religion. They had passed their whole lives in travelling from one chieftain's residence to another, for the purpose of endeavouring to explain away insults, to offer apologies, and to strive by every means in their power to establish peace between those about to plunge their country into the horrors of war. I have several times met these benevolent men journeying through the country on these pacific missions; and twice during my residence here they have been the happy means of preventing bloodshed. Although the New Zealander is so fond of war, and possesses such war-like manners, yet are these peacemakers held in the highest respect, although they do not hold any sacred function—indeed, no order of priesthood exists amongst the natives. I have never discovered any symptoms of religion in these people, except it consists in a great variety of absurd and superstitious ceremonies. Before I visited this island I used to imagine, from seeing so great a variety of carved figures which had been brought from this country, that they were idols, to whom they paid their devotions; but in this I was deceived. They were merely the grotesque carvings of rude artists, possessing a lively fancy, and were a proof of their industry as well as genius. Every chief's house is adorned with an abundance of these carved monsters. One of their favourite subjects is a lizard taking hold of the top of a man's head; their tradition being that that was the origin of man. The lizard is sacred, and never injured by them. Several of their chiefs assured me they believed in the existence of a great and invisible spirit, called Atna, who keeps a constant charge and watch over them; and that they are constantly looking out for tokens of his approbation or displeasure. There is not a wind that blows but they imagine it bears some message from him. And there are not wanting crafty men who pretend to a much more intimate knowledge of his sentiments than the generality, and they easily work on the minds of the credulous and the ignorant. These imposters obtain great consideration, and their counsel and advice is most anxiously sought after by those about to undertake any important business; but, like ancient astrologers and modern gypsies, they speak only in ambiguous terms; so that whatever may be the result, their prediction may still correspond with it.

Like all rude and ignorant people, the New Zealanders seem more to fear the wrath of their God than to love his attributes; and constant sacrifices (too often human ones) are offered up to appease his anger. They imagine that the just and glorious Deity is ever ready to destroy, and that His hand is always stretched forth to execute vengeance.

These sacred, or, more correctly speaking, these "cunning" men and women, who pretend to see into futurity, and to hold an intercourse with the Great Spirit, are here (in one way, at least) turned to a good and useful account. As they themselves are held sacred, everything they wish to have taken particular care of, they can render sacred also. All the chiefs find these people of the greatest use in protecting their property, for they possess the power of tabooing, and when once this ceremony is performed over any person or thing, no one dares to touch either; and for a sufficiently good bribe they will impart their sacred power to any chief, who, by means of this device, thus can protect a field of potatoes or grain, at fifty miles distance from his settlement, more securely and effectually than by any fences, or number of persons he might place to guard it.

This ceremony of taboo, which is common to the whole of the South Sea Islands, seems the principal part of their religion, and it is really difficult to walk without trespassing or infringing on some spot under this influence. All those who touch a corpse are immediately taboo'd, and must be fed like an infant, as their own hands must not touch anything that is put into their mouths. In fact, as we strolled through the village at the time of their evening repast, it appeared as though some dreadful disease had suddenly struck the greater part of the inhabitants, and deprived them of the use of their limbs, most of them being either fed by their slaves, or lying flat down on the ground, and with their mouths eating out of their platters or baskets. The canoe that carries a corpse to the place of its interment is, from that time, taboo'd and laid up; and if any one by chance touches it, he does so at his peril.

All those chiefs who were under the operating hands of Aranghie, the tatooer, were under this law, and all those who worked upon their war canoes were similarly situated. Unfortunately for me, I one day took away a handful of chips from their dockyard to make our fire burn clearly. I was informed they were taboo'd, and upon my pleading ignorance, and sorrow for the misdemeanour, together with a promise not to renew the offence, I was pardoned. A poor hen of ours did not escape so well; she, poor thing, ventured to form a nest, and actually hatched a fine family of chickens amongst these sacred shavings! Loud was the outcry, and great the horror she occasioned when she marched forth cackling, with her merry brood around her. She and "all her little ones" were sacrificed instantly. What became of their bodies we could never learn; probably the workmen were not too fastidious to eat them.

I have observed, since my residence here, one circumstance which proves a kind feeling in the natives, and shows they are not averse to the preaching of the missionaries, or the doctrines they inculcate.

It was the custom of all the Europeans settled here, on the beach at Kororarika, to refrain from all kinds of work on the Sabbath; to shave, and dress themselves in their best habiliments; and if any of the missionaries came over, they went forth to meet them, and hear divine service. Several of the natives generally assembled and witnessed the ceremony; and as they observed it came every seventh day, they called it "the white taboo'd day, when the pakeha (or white men) put on clean clothes, and leave off work;" and, strange to say, the natives also abstained from working on that day. Nothing could induce them to the contrary; not that we wished to persuade them to work, but merely endeavoured so to do to ascertain the strength of their politeness. Not a bit of work would they do upon a Sunday, although it was a critical time with them; for all the chiefs were unprepared with their war canoes for the approaching expedition. At length we discovered that their cunning was as conspicuous as their politeness. They had observed we generally lay longer in bed on a Sunday morning than any other; they accordingly were up by break of day, and had completed many hours' work before we made our appearance; but the moment one of us did appear the work was instantly left off. This degree of outward respect, though craftily managed, was infinitely more than could be reasonably expected from a rude and turbulent savage. It is mere respect than we Europeans pay to any religious ceremony we do not understand. Even their taboo'd grounds would not be so respected by us, if we were not quite certain they possessed the power instantly to revenge any affront offered to their sacred places.

Of all animals introduced by the Europeans, the most unserviceable, and indeed injurious, have been the dogs. They have increased rapidly; every spot was crowded with poor half-starved curs, that were all night long committing depredations on the poultry, pigs, and goats; and if some effectual means of diminishing this pernicious breed is not soon resorted to, the island will be cleared of every other quadruped. Goats were beginning to increase, and the craggy heights round the bays formed a favourite retreat for these interesting wanderers. Captain Duke put himself to great expense and trouble, and effected the importation of some sheep from Van Diemen's Land; but the dogs soon destroyed them all.

THE MASSACRE OF THE FRENCH NAVIGATOR MARION AND PARTY

Our friend George generally paid us a visit after the business of the day was over, and took a cup of tea; wine or grog he detested: so, while he sipped his beverage, we lit our pipes, and managed, with our slight knowledge of his language, together with his imperfect English, to keep up a sort of conversation. Sometimes this was rather wearisome; but occasionally it became interesting in the extreme. He told us that, when Captain Cook touched here, he was a little child; but that his mother (old Turero, who was then with him) remembered his coming well. The French navigator, Marion, he recollected perfectly, and made one of the party that murdered him and his people. His observation was, "They were all brave men; but they were killed and eaten."

He assured us that the catastrophe was quite unpremeditated. Marion's entire ignorance of the customs of the New Zealanders occasioned that distressing event: as I have before observed, that strangers, not acquainted with their religious prejudices, are likely to commit some fatal error; and no action is more likely to lead a party into danger than an incautious use of the seine, for most of the beaches (best suited for that purpose) are taboo'd. This led to the dreadful fate of Marion and his party. I understood from George, that when Marion's men assembled to trail their net on the sacred beach, the natives used every kind of entreaty and remonstrance to induce them to forbear, but, either from ignorance or obstinacy, they persisted in their intentions, and drew their net to land.

The natives, greatly incensed by this act of impiety, vowed revenge; and the suspicions of the French not being roused, an opportunity soon presented itself of taking ample retaliation. The seine being very heavy, the French required the assistance of the natives in drawing it on shore. These wily fellows instantly consented to the task, and placed themselves alternately between each Frenchman, apparently, to equalise the work. Consequently, in the act of pulling, each native had a white man before him; and, on an appointed signal, the brains of each European were knocked out by a tremendous blow of the stone hatchet.

Captain Marion, who, from his ship, was an eye-witness of these horrid murders, instantly hastened on shore with the remainder of his crew to avenge the slaughter of his countrymen. Led on more by ardour than prudence, he suffered himself to be surrounded; was overpowered by numbers, defeated, and every one was put to death!

This account of George's does not, I acknowledge, exactly agree with the published narrative of that unfortunate event, nor does his age agree with the dates. Only a few years elapsed between the time of Cook and Marion, yet he declares himself to have been a child at the death of the navigator, and a man at the murder of the latter; but as it was voluntary on his part to give me the above detail, and even if he were not present himself, he most probably had the facts from one who was, I thought it worth inserting, as tending to throw light on one of the most melancholy events which ever took place on these coasts.

George also related to me the dreadful tragedy of the ship Boyd, and, horrible as these relations were, I felt a particular interest, almost amounting to pleasure, in hearing them related by an eye-witness; one who had been an actor in those bloody scenes which I had before read of: narratives which from my very childhood had always possessed particular charms for me; and at this time I was not only looking on the very spot the hero of my imagination, Cook, had trod, but was hearing the tale from one who had actually seen him; and was listening to every particular concerning the transactions of Marion and his men, as though they had just taken place.

Even in the dreadful destruction of the Boyd, George laid the blame entirely on the English, and spoke with great bitterness of the ill-treatment of Philip, the native chief, who came as passenger in the ship. He described and mimicked his cleaning shoes and knives; his being flogged when he refused to do this degrading work; and, finally, his speech to his countrymen when he came on shore, soliciting their assistance in capturing the vessel, and revenging his ill-treatment. Over and over again our friend George, having worked up his passion by a full recollection of the subject, went through the whole tragedy. The scene thus portrayed was interesting although horrible. No actor, trained in the strictest rules of his art, could compete with George's vehemence of action. The flexibility of his features enabled him to vary the expression of each passion; and he represented hatred, anger, horror, and the imploring of mercy so ably that, in short, one would have imagined he had spent his whole life in practising the art of imitation.

CHAPTER XXXIV

THE MAORI VIEW OF CHRISTIANITY

I frequently conversed with George upon the subject of religion, and from what he told me I found that the natives had not formed the slightest idea of there being a state of future punishment. They refuse to believe that the good Spirit intends to make them miserable after their decease. They imagine all the actions of this life are punished here, and that every one when dead, good or bad, bondsman or free, is assembled on an island situated near the North Cape, where both the necessaries and comforts of life will be found in the greatest abundance, and all will enjoy a state of uninterrupted happiness. A people of their simple habits, and possessing so little property, have but few temptations to excesses of any kind, excepting the cruelties practised by them in war, in which they fancy themselves perfectly justified, and the tyranny exercised by them over their slaves, whom they look upon as mere machines. There is, in fact, but little crime among them, for which reason they cannot imagine any man wicked enough to deserve eternal punishment. This opinion of theirs we saw an illustration of one Sunday, when one of the missionaries paid us a visit.

The ceremony of all assembling to public worship astonished the natives greatly, though they always behaved with the utmost decorum when admitted into the house where the ceremony takes place. On the day in question the minister endeavoured to explain the sacred mysteries of our religion to a number of the chiefs who were present. They listened attentively to all he said, and expressed no doubts as to its truth, only remarking that "as all these wonderful circumstances happened only in the country of the white men, the great Spirit expected the white men only to believe them." The missionary then began to expatiate on the torments of hell, at which some of them seemed horrified, but others said "they were quite sure such a place could only be made for the white faces, for they had no men half wicked enough in New Zealand to be sent there;" but when the reverend gentleman added with vehemence that "all men" would be condemned, the savages all burst into a loud laugh, declaring "they would have nothing to do with a God who delighted in such cruelties; and then (as a matter of right) hoped the missionary would give them each a blanket for having taken the trouble of listening to him so patiently."

I cannot forbear censuring the missionaries, inasmuch as they prevent the natives, by every means in their power, from acquiring the English language. They make a point of mastering the native tongue as quickly as possible, and being able to give their whole time and attention to it, this is easily accomplished. It is of importance that they should do so, otherwise they could not carry on the duties of the mission; but by thus engrossing the knowledge, they obtain great influence over the minds of the natives. We ourselves were sadly puzzled by a correspondence we had with two native chiefs, who had been taught to read and write by some of the Society; but their acquirements being in their native language, were of no possible use. The difficulty of teaching them English would not have been greater, and then what stores of information and improvement might not their instructors have laid open to them.

CHAPTER XXXV

THREATENED INVASION BY HONGI

We had passed some months here, and were beginning to look out for the return of our brig, to take us again into civilised society, when we were once more thrown into alarm by a threatened invasion. A rumour was circulated in the village that Hongi, who now lay at the point of death, had declared that he would make one last glorious effort before he expired. He was resolved (it was reported) to collect his warriors, overcome George and his followers, possess himself of Kororarika, and die upon the conquered territory of his enemy; and I had no doubt that in his moment of delirium such had been his exclamations, as it had always been one of his favourite projects. When this was reported to George, he immediately came to us, and with a most doleful countenance told us we must take care of ourselves; for, if the report proved true, he was much too weak to protect us. This certainly caused us some alarm, but, fortunately for us, a good-sized whaler, the Marianne, was then lying at anchor in the port, having arrived but a few days previously. The presence of a ship, all over the world, is felt as a protection to Europeans, as in case of danger it is a sure place of refuge.

King George sent off his messengers in every direction to inform his friends and dependants of the threats uttered against him by Hongi, and the next day eight large war canoes, filled with warriors, came to his assistance. They landed at some distance from the beach, and, as it was late in the day, they would not make their public *entree* till the next morning; for the New Zealanders are very fond of giving a grand effect to all their public meetings. I determined to pay them a visit, to witness the ceremonies of the night bivouack, which proved a most picturesque scene, and wild and beautiful in the extreme. Their watch fires glanced upon the dark skins of these finely formed men, and on their bright weapons. Some groups were dancing; others were lying round a fire, chanting wild songs, descriptive of former wars; whilst the graver elders sat in a circle, and discussed the present state of affairs. All were delighted to see me, and each group offered to share their fire and provisions with the "white visitor," as they termed me.

The next morning these auxiliary forces were seen descending the hills to our village; and, in order to return the compliment, we all went in our best array to receive them. There were upwards of two hundred athletic, naked savages, each armed with his firelock, and marching with the utmost regularity. The chiefs took the lead. The alarm such a sight might have created was dissipated by the certainty that they came as our protectors. I even imagined their countenances were not so ferocious as usual but as they approached near to our party, the usual sham fight began, accompanied by the war dance, and although I expected it, and indeed had come for the purpose of witnessing it, it was conducted with so much fury on both sides, that at length I became quite horrified, and for some time could not divest myself of the feeling that our visitors were playing false, so closely did this mock combat resemble a real one. The dreadful noises, the hideous faces, the screeching of the women, and the menacing gestures of each party, were so calculated to inspire terror, that stouter hearts than mine might have felt fear. When the tumult subsided, the elder chiefs squatted down, and had the long talk usual on these occasions.

I was much delighted to recognise among these chiefs one I had known at Sydney. During his residence in that city I had permitted him to remain in my house, and the few presents which he had requested on his return to his own country I had provided him with, and sent him off delighted and happy, and never expected to behold him again. The moment I approached he recollected me, jumped up from the "council," ran up to me, hugged me in his arms, and rubbed noses so forcibly with me that I felt his friendship for some time, besides being daubed all over most plentifully with red ochre, which he, being then on a war-like and ceremonious visit, was smeared with from head to foot.

When my savage friend (whom we used to call Mr. Tookee) had overcome his first burst of delight at seeing me, and had literally left off jumping for joy, he introduced me to his father, Mr. De Frookee, the chief of his tribe, a very fine specimen of an old New Zealander, who was (I found) highly respected for his integrity and benevolence. His eyes overflowed with tears when he heard I was the person who had shown such kindness to his son at Sydney. I soon felt quite "at home" with the old chief, and experienced the good effect of having kept my word with this uncultivated savage. I had, at the time I presented him with the gifts, been much laughed at by my acquaintances at Sydney for putting myself to such unnecessary expense; but, from the gratitude he displayed for the trifling services I had then rendered him, I felt assured he and his companions would do all in their power to protect me from every danger.

A long discussion was now carried on, one speaker at a time occupying the oblong space round which the warriors sat, and the more animated the debate, the faster ran the speaker to and fro, flourishing his hatchet in a most dexterous manner. The instant one speaker finishes, another starts up to answer him; but previous to rising they throw a mat or blanket over their shoulders, and arrange it most tastefully around them; and, as their attitudes are all striking and graceful, and a great part of the figure is left exposed, it forms a study for an artist, well worth his going many miles to witness, and invariably reminded me of the fine models of antiquity.

As a painter, I conceive that this must have been the great secret of the perfection to which the Greek and Roman sculptors brought their works; as they constantly contemplated the display of the human form in all its beauty in their various gymnastic exercises, which enabled them to transfer to marble such ease and elegance as we, living in an age of coats and breeches, never shall be able to rival.

After the important subjects had been settled by the elders, the young men assembled without their weapons, and began another kind of sham fight, one grappling with another, till hundreds of them were locked in each other's arms, and were flung in heaps in every direction. After they were tired of this pastime, a regular ring was formed, and a wrestling match began, which was carried on in as regular and fair a manner as a boxing match in our own country, and as much skill and cunning were displayed in the art of throwing as the greatest connoisseur would desire. I was pleased, also, to observe that, whatever happened (and some most severe throws and blows passed), nothing could disturb their good humour.

This party, having remained for seven days on our beach, and not hearing anything more of our intended invaders, their provisions also becoming rather scarce, took leave in order to return to their own district, placing scouts to give them quick intelligence of the movements of the enemy.

CHAPTER XXXVI

ARRIVAL OF A WARSHIP

A few days after the departure of this friendly tribe, a "King's ship" of eighteen guns arrived in the Bay; consequently all our fears of an immediate invasion were over. No sooner had she cast anchor than our friend George came to us, expressing the greatest anxiety to visit King George of England's warship, and requesting we would accompany him, which we readily agreed to do; and he left us to adorn himself for the occasion. Soon after he reappeared in great state. A very splendid war-mat was thrown over his shoulders; his hair was dressed, oiled, and decorated with feathers, and his person was plentifully covered with red ochre: he appeared a very fine-looking fellow: his mother, his three wives, and all his sons and daughters were dressed in equal magnificence, and accompanied him.

In this state we went off to visit the vessel; but the moment I came alongside, I repented my being there, for the rude and churlish manner in which we were received distressed me considerably. In the first place, an order was given that none but the chief himself should be allowed to come on board; consequently his wives and daughters were obliged to remain in the canoe. The captain spoke only a few words to George, who was allowed to remain but a few minutes in the cabin; on getting up to take leave, George took off his fine war-mantle and presented it to the captain; but, receiving no other covering in return for his gift, he went on shore naked! The officers of the vessel behaved differently: they conducted us all down into the gun-room, where they treated us most kindly, and paid every attention to our friend George, whose dignity was deeply wounded by the cool and contemptuous behaviour of the captain.

How greatly is it to be regretted that some arrangements are not made by our Government at Home, and that there are not orders given to commanders of ships of war touching here to pay attention to the chiefs, and to make some trifling presents amongst them; for there never were a people more anxious to cultivate a friendly intercourse with British subjects than the inhabitants of New Zealand: and yet there is scarcely a Government vessel that puts into port here but the natives receive some insult, though they are sent for the express purpose of supporting the dignity of the English nation, and to cultivate the amicable feelings of the chiefs.

When a "King's ship" comes to anchor, the chiefs (with all the glee of children going to a fair) collect together their wives, children, and friends, and pay a visit to the "fighting ships," to see King George's warriors (as they call them): when they come alongside they are kept off by an armed sentry; and, after a long parley, they are informed the chief may come, but his family and friends must not. In this case, the natives generally spit at the vessel, and, uttering execrations on their inhospitality, return on shore.

One of the savage chieftains who accompanied us to the vessel in question, on our way back remarked, "that the white warriors were *afraid* of admitting them, though they were unarmed and but a few; while the warriors in the ships were many, and armed with their great guns."

Living entirely amongst these people so long as I had done, I felt the absurdity of such conduct, and the folly of treating them so harshly. If ever individuals are so situated as to need either the esteem or the confidence of savages, they must bear with their prying and childish curiosity, and not be afraid of treating them too kindly; by this means they become the quietest and gentlest creatures in the world; but, if treated with contumely, and their wives and families repulsed from your ship, they become dangerous, vindictive, and cruel neighbours, as many a dreadful deed which has taken place in this vicinity will fully prove.

CHAPTER XXXVII

THE WHALERS AND THE MISSIONARIES

The South Sea whalers are the ships the natives are the most anxious to see on their coasts; and it is the crews of those vessels who have, in a manner, civilised these hardy islanders. Captain Gardiner, of the Marianne (the vessel now in the harbour), is the oldest person in that trade; and he informed me, that not longer than twenty years back scarcely any vessel would dare to touch at New Zealand; and when, from particular circumstances, they were obliged so to do, they kept their boarding-nettings up, and kept a strict guard night and day: their fears arose from a want of knowledge of the disposition of the people. The vessels frequenting the island use no precautions now: hundreds of natives are permitted to crowd on board each ship; and no accident has ever occurred from this mode of treatment. But when a ship of war arrives here for the first time, the precautions taken are, to arm the row-guard with cutlasses and pistols, and to harass the crew with constant watching, while the only enemy that exists is in their own imaginations. To the courage and enterprise of the commanders of whalers all credit is due for working the rapid change in these once bloody-minded savages, and forming safe and commodious harbours for their vessels to refit in: this have they done in a part of the world lately looked upon with horror. What credit soever the missionaries may take to themselves, or try to make their supporters in England believe, every man who has visited this place, and will speak his mind freely and disinterestedly, must acknowledge *they* have had no share in bringing about this change of character; but, on the contrary, they have done all that in them lay to injure the reputation of the whaler in the estimation of the natives. Hitherto they have not succeeded: their want of hospitality and kindness to their own countrymen raises a strong dislike to them in the minds of these unsophisticated people. According to their simple notions of right and wrong, they think the want of hospitality an unpardonable offence, and that the counsel or advice of a man who shuts his door against his neighbour is not worthy of being attended to.

I will give the reader one more anecdote of these men, who are sent out to set an example of the beauty of the Christian faith to the unenlightened heathens. A few weeks since, the festival of Christmas took place; and Englishmen, in whatever part of the world they chance to be, make a point of assembling together on that day, our recollections then being associated with "home" and our families, uniting to spend that day in mutual congratulations and wishes for happiness. For some time previous to its arrival, the captains of the two whalers and myself had been deliberating where we should spend this social day; and it was finally settled that we should cross the bay to Te Puna, a beautiful and romantic spot, the residence of an intelligent chief, called Warri Pork, and an Englishman, named Hanson. Near this was a church missionary establishment; and at this Englishman's house we determined we would spend the day. The captains of the two whalers then in the harbour joined our party; and as everyone contributed his share towards our picnic feast, the joint stock made altogether a respectable appearance.

We proceeded to Te Puna in two whaleboats: it was a most delightful trip, the scenery being strikingly beautiful. The village of Ranghe Hue, belonging to Warri Pork, is situated on the summit of an immense and abrupt hill: the huts belonging to the savages appeared, in many places, as though they were overhanging the sea, the height being crowned with a mighty pah. At the bottom of this hill, and in a beautiful valley, the cottages of the missionaries are situated, complete pictures of English comfort, content, and prosperity; they are close to a bright sandy beach: a beautiful green slope lies in their rear, and a clear and never-failing stream of water runs by the side of their enclosures. As the boats approached this lovely spot, I was in an ecstasy of delight: such a happy mixture of savage and civilised life I had never seen before; and when I observed the white smoke curling out of the chimneys of my countrymen, I anticipated the joyful surprise, the hearty welcome, the smiling faces, and old Christmas compliments that were going to take place, and the great pleasure it would give our secluded countrymen to meet us, in these distant regions, at this happy season, and talk of our relatives and friends in England.

My romantic notions were soon crushed; our landing gave no pleasure to these secluded Englishmen: they gave us no welcome; but, as our boats approached the shore, they walked away to their own dwellings, closed their gates and doors after them, and gazed at us through their windows; and during three days that we passed in a hut quite near them, they never exchanged one word with any of the party. Thus foiled in our hopes of spending a social day with our compatriots, after our dinner was over we sent materials for making a bowl of punch up the hill to the chiefs, and spent the remainder of the day surrounded by generous savages, who were delighted with our company, and who did everything in their power to make us comfortable. In the course of the afternoon two of the mission came up to preach; but the savages were so angry with them for not showing more kindness to their own countrymen, that none would listen to them.

I have visited many of the Roman Catholic missionary establishments; their priests adopt quite a different line of conduct: they are cheerful and kind to the savage pagan, and polite and attentive to their European brethren; they have gained the esteem of those they have been sent to convert; they have introduced their own language amongst them, which enables them to have intercourse with strangers; and, however we may differ in some tenets of religious belief, we must acknowledge the success of their mission. They have brought nearly the whole of the Indian population in South America into the bosom of their church; and their converts form the greater part of the people. Notwithstanding the numerous church and sectarian missionaries sent from England, I never met with one Indian converted by them. I have attended mass in an Indian village; a native priest performed the ceremony, and the whole congregation (except myself) were of his cast and complexion: and, it is worthy of remark, that in Peru, and some of the most populous provinces, a pagan is scarcely to be found.

CHAPTER XXXVIII

THREATENED WAR

We now heard that Tetoro (one of the most powerful chiefs of this part of the island) had taken offence, and had sent a defiance to King George, saying he intended coming to seek revenge, accompanied by a strong body of warriors; and the "herald" who brought this proclamation informed us that the English settlers were to be attacked and plundered also.

We had every reason to fear this might prove a more calamitous affair than any we had yet experienced; as George immediately collected all his family and dependents, and took his departure for the Kawakawa river (the residence of De Kookie, the chief who had come to his assistance against Hongi's attack), leaving behind only a few slaves. Thus a second time were we left to our own resources on Kororarika Beach. George and his followers were too much scattered: some were trading with the ships, others were distributed in various districts, attending to their agricultural pursuits. Thus separated, each might become an easy prey to any of the powerful chiefs; but, were they united, they would be too strong for any of the tribes: unfortunately the hope of gain made them risk so great a danger. At this period, too, there was not a single vessel in the bay to protect us. The known partiality of all the tribes for Europeans was the only consolation we had; and we endeavoured to cheer each other with this hope, under what in reality might be considered very appalling circumstances.

After enduring this state of suspense and anxiety for several days, and no enemy appearing, we determined to pay a visit to the camp of the combined army of our friends, which would, at the same time, gratify our own curiosity, and give them a degree of satisfaction; as it would prove to them that we were not afraid of venturing amongst them, even in times of danger. We accordingly prepared the whaleboats to proceed up the Kawakawa river; and, as I had never been there before, the present afforded an excellent opportunity for exploring that picturesque spot.

At the top of the Bay of Islands, two rivers disembogue, the Wye Catte and the Kawakawa: they are both small but beautiful streams. It was early in the morning when we started: the dewy mist rose from the unruffled bosom of the river like the gradual lifting up of a curtain, and, at length, displayed its lofty sides, covered with immense trees, the verdure extending to the very edge of the water. All was quiet, beautiful, and serene; the only sounds which broke the calm were the wild notes of the tui (or New Zealand blackbird), the splashing of our own oars, or the occasional flight of a wild duck (or shag), disturbed by our approach.

We rowed our boat many miles without seeing the slightest vestige of any human inhabitants or civilisation: all appeared wild and magnificent as if just fresh from the hands of nature; and it failed not to lead the mind up to the contemplation of the Creator. It seemed utterly impossible to reconcile the idea that such lonely, romantic, and sequestered scenes could conceal hordes of savage cannibals, or that the tranquility of this very place would soon be exchanged for the noise and tumult of savage warfare. We soon reached the village where the coalesced chiefs had taken up their station: they had fortified their position, and were waiting the approach of the enemy. No sooner, however, was our arrival known, than all came running down tumultuously to give us welcome: all business was laid aside to greet our landing, and we were conducted with great ceremony into the centre of the camp.

CHAPTER XXXIX

CONSTRUCTION OF A PA

We found eight hundred warriors, who (to use a sea phrase) were "all at quarters." The magic pen of Scott might here have been well employed to describe "The Gathering." The chiefs sat apart from their followers in deep consultation: we did not approach near enough to hear their discussion; but it ended by their paying us a high compliment for coming amongst them. The young and active were busily employed in constructing a strong stockade fort to annoy the enemy as he approached; others were preparing their weapons, or practising the use of arms.

The village itself was an object of extreme interest; and, after contemplating the war-like preparations of the chiefs, we turned with pleasure to gaze on the beauty of the surrounding country. In a plain, surrounded by high hills, with a beautiful stream of water meandering through it, was situated a group of huts; and many acres of cultivated ground, neatly fenced and cleared, encircled them. Their harvest, consisting of Indian corn, potatoes, and kumara, was now ready for gathering, and all the women were busily occupied. As I from an eminence looked down upon their labours, I could almost fancy I was in Italy, and beheld the peasantry at work in their vineyards: but the adjacent camp and naked warriors soon dissipated the illusion!

On approaching the village we occasioned quite a commotion: the girls brought forth baskets filled with cooked kumaras and peaches, while the men erected a tent to screen us from the rays of the sun: indeed, all seemed anxious to do something that should prove acceptable to us. We had brought with us sufficient provision for a good dinner which was soon cooked, and we invited them to partake of our fare, and a very merry and noisy group we formed. After our repast, the chief warriors took us round their camp, and exhibited to us all their means of defence, and the different works they had thrown up. Where the use of artillery is unknown, the principles of fortification are simple, and the New Zealanders seem to possess a clear notion of the art: necessity being with them the mother of invention.

In the direction where the approach of the enemy was expected, they had erected a strong square stockade, to molest the army; while the women and children retired to the principal fort, which was very strong, and situated at the summit of the highest hill: it had a breast-work all round it about five feet high, and a broad ditch beyond that. The fortress was large enough to contain several hundred men: it had a spacious glacis in front, and every approach to it was so completely exposed, that we thought even a body of regular troops, without artillery, would have found it very difficult to storm; and to the New Zealand warrior it seemed a wonderful and impregnable work.

The chief who had the command of this fort was our old acquaintance Kiney Kiney, a younger brother of King George's, who seemed proud of this honour, and appeared highly delighted in showing us round, and explaining everything to us; even condescending to ask our advice as to any means of adding strength and security to the works. He listened attentively to all our observations; and if he approved any alteration we suggested he ordered it instantly to be carried into effect. I noticed a thicket too near the fort, and told him I thought it might shelter a body of men, and before I left the pa it was reduced to a heap of ashes. Sentinels were posted in every direction to give notice of the approach of an enemy. *Mr.* Kiney Kiney (as he was sometimes called) was splendidly apparelled on this occasion: he had, by some means or other, become possessed of a light infantry sabre, with all its paraphernalia of belts and buckles; this was girded round his naked body, which gave him a very gallant air, and, I have no doubt, was the envy and admiration of all his followers.

CHAPTER XL

A SHAM FIGHT

After we had seen and approved all their preparations, we were treated with a grand review and sham fight: they divided themselves into two parties; one half the number took their station on a hill, and lay concealed; the other party crouched on the plains to receive the attack, all kneeling on one knee, with their eyes fixed on the spot whence they expected the rush of their pretended enemies. In a moment, the concealed party burst forth from their ambush, with a tremendous and simultaneous shout, and the mock battle began with great fury.

Nothing in nature can be imagined more horrible than the noise they make on these occasions. I have heard, under circumstances of some peril, the North American Indian war-whoop; but that is trifling compared with it and their countenances are hideous beyond description. My principal astonishment on these occasions was, that they did not actually kill each other, or, at least, break each other's bones; for they seemed to strike with all the fury and vigour of a real engagement; but they kept such exact time, that at a moment's notice they all left off, and began joking and laughing, except a very few, whom I observed to sneak away to wash off some bloody witness, or to put a plaster on their broken skin.

After these military and gymnastic exhibitions, they formed a grand assembly, and the chiefs, as usual, made long speeches in rotation. This rude parliament is one of the most beautiful features in savage government: all public matters are discussed openly, grievances are complained of, and justice is summarily administered.

Thus, after spending a pleasant day, we rose to depart, and took an affectionate leave of our entertainers, who were most anxious that we should remain longer; but we thought we had better return to Kororarika, where our property had been left. Most of the chiefs accompanied us to our boats, and, after exhibiting various testimonies of their friendly feeling towards us, they suffered us to depart.

The day following this visit, we were alarmed by the appearance of two war canoes crossing the bay: we waited their approach with considerable anxiety: what few valuables we had with us we concealed about our persons; but, as they neared our beach, our fears subsided, on finding there were only a few men in each. Three chiefs (unarmed) landed, whom we found to be Rivers and two of his near kinsmen, the most dreaded persons of our expected invaders; but they immediately informed us they came on a mission of peace, and, for that reason, had come to us unattended and unarmed.

We were most happy to hear this, and to find hostilities were again likely to be deferred. Though we well knew the character of these men, and that they were capable of the most treacherous acts, and the deepest dissimulation, yet, their thus throwing themselves into our power, with the olive branch in their hands, was irresistible; and we received them with all the pomp we were capable of. We ordered a pig to be killed for the feast, and requested them to remain for that night. In order to do honour to our noble guests, and credit to our friend and ally King George, we produced all the luxuries we had; and, in addition to the pork, piles of pancakes and molasses were devoured: after this we gave them tea, of which they are very fond; and, over our pipes, in the evening, we informed them of the preparations the coalesced chiefs had made for their reception, had their intentions been hostile.

The next morning they embarked for the camp at Kawakawa, where, I understood, they had considerable difficulty in arranging the "treaty of peace": George having been so often alarmed, now that such great preparations had been effected (as he well know the treacherous character of his foe), he was unwilling to give up the hopes of conquest; however, by the advice of the chiefs, it was finally settled amicably. George and his friends accordingly returned to Kororarika, leaving a strong party at the pa to finish the fortifications; and, though peace was made, our party still kept themselves in a posture of defence.

CHAPTER XLI

RETURN OF THE BRIG.—AN EXCITING INCIDENT

We had been expecting with great anxiety the return of our brig; and, soon after the termination of this affair, we had the pleasure of seeing her enter the bay, after her cruise from Tongataboo and Tucopea. We found that, on leaving the Bay of Islands, she had touched at the Thames, or (as the natives call it) Hauraki, in order to land two chiefs, whom Captain Dillon had taken thence two years before, and, in the confusion occasioned by the disembarking, the visiting and congratulations of friends (the vessel being under weigh), one chief was left on board, who had not been discovered till all the canoes were out of sight, and there remained no other alternative for him than to proceed on the whole voyage.

This was of no importance as it respected Tongataboo or Tucopea; but, on his return to Kororarika, it was not only placing him, but all of us, in a dreadful dilemma! His tribe being at deadly enmity with that of George, the moment he was seen on deck (which was as soon as the vessel arrived), George and all the men in the various canoes appeared to grow outrageous: nothing would convince them but that we were in league with their enemies, and had brought this spy into their territories from interested motives; and they seemed resolved upon boarding the brig and executing vengeance upon the unfortunate victim. To all our remonstrances George replied, "Any other man than this I would have pardoned; but it was only last year he killed, and helped to eat, my own uncle, whose death still remains unrevenged: I cannot allow him to leave my country alive; if I did, I should be despised for ever."

I was greatly grieved at the circumstance; but, as I was somewhat of a favourite with George, I succeeded in convincing him that it arose purely from accident, and no intention of giving him offence; and he consented to leave him on board, but cautioned us not to allow him to land. "If I see him on shore he dies," he repeated several times. It would have been well for us had we attended to this warning: we did not; and we accordingly infringed on the customs of his country; thus placing ourselves in a most perilous situation with the natives, and plainly showing that the imprudence of our countrymen is invariably the cause of quarrels and misunderstandings with these islanders.

Some days having passed since this altercation with George, we thought no more about it. The brig, from various causes, was certain to remain some time in this harbour; and, as our New Zealand guest expressed a great desire to go on shore one day, we consented to his accompanying us. We had scarcely entered our house, when we had reason to repent the imprudent step we had taken: all the natives were in commotion; messengers were sent off to George to acquaint him with the circumstance, and soon after we saw him, attended by all his relations, accoutred for war; that is, quite naked, their skins oiled and painted, and armed with muskets. Fury was in their looks and gestures as they hastened towards our residence. We had scarcely time to shut and fasten our door, when they made a rush to force it; and we had a severe struggle to keep them out. At one period their rage became so ungovernable that we expected every instant they would fire on us for preventing their entrance. The man who was the cause of all this violence crept into our bedroom, and kept out of sight; but he did not, at any period of the disturbance, exhibit the least sign of fear, so accustomed are they from childhood to these deadly frays.

When the natives found we would not give up the man, but that they must murder us before they could accomplish their revenge, the disappointment rendered them nearly frantic. Our situation was most critical and appalling; and nothing can be a more convincing proof of the influence the Europeans have obtained over them, than that, at such a moment, they should have refrained from setting fire to or pulling down the house, and sacrificing every one of us. George again remonstrated with us, assuring us it was his sacred duty to destroy this man, now he was in his territory; a duty which, he said, he owed to the memory of his murdered relations, and which must be performed, even though he should sacrifice his "good English friends." He cautioned us not to stand between him and his enemy, who must die before the sun set, pointing, at the same time, to that luminary, and ordering his slaves to kindle a large fire to roast him on. Finally, he and his friends planted themselves all round the house to prevent the escape of their victim. Thus were we environed with fifty or sixty well armed and exasperated savages.

Our imprudence had given us no other alternative than either to give up the man, who had put himself under our protection, or still to defend him at the risk of our own lives: we instantly adopted the latter course. Fortunately for us, a whaler was lying in the harbour, and a party of her men were then on shore in the neighbourhood procuring water. We had sent to them to explain the nature of our situation, and we saw them coming to our assistance, though the numbers of natives at this time assembled totally precluded all chance of our getting off by force; and a variety of schemes were suggested as to how we should save the man's life, and get clear of this difficulty, without sacrificing the good opinion we were held in by the natives.

We were well aware of the great importance it was to George to continue on friendly terms with the English vessels touching here, as they not only afforded him various sources of considerable profit, but the intercourse gave him great importance in the eyes of his countrymen; and we determined to make this circumstance a means of saving the man's life, as we suspected that a threat of removing the seat of trade would soon make him compromise his revenge for his interest.

We therefore sent him a formal message, that, if he was resolved to kill his enemy in our house, we had determined not to prevent him, but that we would not stay to witness such a cruelty; and that we should immediately remove every thing we possessed on board ship, leave the Bay of Islands, and seek the protection and shelter of some other chief; and, if he compelled us to do so, no other British ship would ever be seen at Kororarika.

We accordingly ordered the ship's boats ashore, and our things were quickly conveyed into them. I trembled when I looked on the natives, and saw the rage depicted on their countenances; and I, trusting in Providence to avert from me the dreadful death with which I saw myself threatened, prepared myself for some fatal catastrophe. Tumultuous discussions ensued, and it at length became difficult for the elders to restrain the impetuosity of the younger chiefs. Fortunately for us, their vehement speeches soon produced a violent feud amongst themselves. Mutual upbraidings took place: each accused the other of being the cause of quarrel, and the consequent loss of the white men. This was precisely the state of things we wished for; and, while we were waiting the return of the last boat, a messenger came from the elder chiefs, to propose an amicable adjustment of the affair. The chiefs promised that, if we would reland our goods and remain with them, the man we protected should go without molestation on board the brig; but, if we persevered in leaving them, the man should be killed before our eyes. This was what we expected; and though I really now wished to leave them, being quite tired of these perpetual broils, we assented, in order that the man's life might be spared When they found we agreed to their proposal, they retreated out of sight, thereby carefully avoiding polluting their eyes by looking upon their enemy.

No sooner had they disappeared than I visited the poor fellow who had been the cause of all this disturbance: he seemed half dead with anxiety; but I soon revived him with the information that all was settled amicably; and we lost no time in getting him off, which we safely accomplished, though, as the boat which conveyed him left the shore, a bullet whizzed close by me, aimed, no doubt, by some young fiery chief, who had concealed himself in the bushes for that purpose.

During this transaction I witnessed the natural kindness of heart and disinterested tenderness of the female sex: no matter how distressing the circumstance or appalling the danger, they are, in all countries, the last to forsake man. While the enraged chiefs were yelling outside our house, and all our exertions could scarcely prevent them from making a forcible entry, all the women were sitting with, and trying to comfort the unhappy cause of this calamity. They had cooked for him a delicate dinner, brought him fruit, and were using every means by which they could keep up his spirits and buoy up his hopes, confidently assuring him the white men would not yield him up to his ferocious foes. Notwithstanding all their exertions, he was miserable, till informed by me of his safety; and I received the warmest thanks, and even blessings, from his "fair" friends, as if I had conferred upon each a personal favour.

The man being now in safety, we determined to demand satisfaction for the affront which had been put upon us, and we sent George word we could not again receive him into our house unless he made an ample apology for his behaviour, painting in strong colours how deeply our feelings had been wounded, and how much this indignity had lowered us in the esteem of all our acquaintances.

After some consultation among their leading men upon the subject of our message, King George presented himself at the door of our hut, and, in the most humble manner, surrendered his musket; and shortly after his brother Kiney Kiney did the same. Thus we gained our point, and received both payment and apologies for their violent behaviour. Friendship being thus restored, we soon gave them back their muskets, to their infinite surprise and satisfaction.

On reflection, I felt quite convinced that the natives liked us the better for what we had done: it afforded them also a lesson of humanity, for they all well knew we had no other object in view when we stood forward to defend the poor fellow, who had relied upon our promise of protecting him. Several chiefs told us that they greatly admired our principles, and should always feel themselves quite safe with men like us, who would risk their own lives rather than break their word, or desert a friend in the hour of danger.

At the close of this eventful day we received another token of peace, which was in its manner simple and affecting, and not such as could have been expected from a nation of savages. A procession of young girls approached our door, each bearing a basket: some were filled with nicely cooked potatoes, others with various fruits and flowers, which they set down before us, chanting, in a low voice, a song in praise of our recent exploit; a man bearing a very large fish closed the procession; he repeated the song also. We were informed that these presents had been sent by King George as a ratification of friendship, for the New Zealanders never think a reconciliation perfected till you have again eaten and drank with them.

Two important conclusions may be drawn from the termination of this affair: first, that if a spirited interference takes place on the part of the Europeans, murder may be at times prevented, as we actually rescued a mortal foe from the vengeance of an exasperated enemy; and, secondly, their efforts to restore amity proves their extreme desire to have white people settle amongst them.

About a week after this event we witnessed a most extraordinary ceremony, which partook more of the ludicrous than the horrible, though I have no doubt it was regarded by the natives as a most solemn affair. For some days we had been honoured by the presence of a great priest, or one of their chief tabooers; he came for the purpose of discussing with the chiefs the affairs of the nation, particularly the approaching war with the tribe of the Thames; and the day set apart for the discussion of the principal points was ushered in by a rich feast, not of pork nor fish, nor even the kumara, but of two old, sturdy, large dogs!

I was much surprised on rising one morning to see Kiney Kiney, with several chiefs of the highest rank, stripped, and performing the offices of the meanest slave (the washing the feet of the pilgrims by cardinals and persons of rank in Rome came instantly to my remembrance). These chiefs were making a fire and cooking. I was still more astonished, on approaching them, to find the nature of the food they were singeing and scraping. This bow-wow meat they were preparing after the fashion of pork: pigs being the only quadruped they have ever seen cooked, they of course are not acquainted with any other way of dressing the animal creation, and a sad bungling job they made of it; for the dogs were old and tough, and the hair adhered most pertinaciously to the skin, and in many places would not come off.

There were only five persons allowed to partake of this delicious meal, which was, as well as the five partakers, strictly taboo'd for the whole of that day: and we strongly recommended them to hold a similar feast every day, until they had cleared the country of these canine nuisances, the dogs being the greatest pests they have.

CHAPTER XLII

WAR-LIKE EXPEDITION TO THE THAMES

One morning I was roused out of a sound sleep by continued discharges of musketry from a number of war canoes. I jumped up instantly in alarm; but I soon discovered them to be Atoi and his party, who had been absent about two months on a war-like expedition to the Thames, and they were now returning successful.

I had witnessed the departure of this expedition, and considered it in the light of a reconnoitring party. I could not make out what the real object was they had been in search of; but, wherever they had been, they had been victorious, for they now returned with quantities of plunder, human heads, human flesh, and many prisoners! After the dance and sham fight had been duly gone through, they proceeded to land their cargo of spoil. First came a group of miserable creatures, women and children, torn by violence from their native homes, henceforth to be the slaves of their conquerors; some were miserably wounded and lacerated, others looked half-starved, but all seemed wretched and dejected.

The women of Kororarika, with their usual humanity, instantly surrounded them, and endeavoured to console them, and then shed abundance of tears over them. I enquired of one of the warriors what they had done with the male prisoners: he coolly replied, they had all been eaten, except some "titbits," which had been packed up in the baskets and brought on shore, in order to regale particular friends and favourites!

They had also brought with them several heads, which they have the art of preparing in their native ovens, so as not to disfigure the countenance nor injure the figure tatoo'd upon them. One of these, the skull of a distinguished chief, seemed to afford them amazing delight. Most of our people had known him well, and several of his near relations were present: but cruel war seemed to have eradicated every feeling of humanity; for all appeared to contemplate this ghastly object with great satisfaction. These heads were decorated profusely with yellow and red ribbons, and with white feathers: they were then stuck upon short poles, and placed, with great ceremony, in front of the old Queen Turero's house; who, sitting at the door, received this token of respect with approval and condescension.

The group altogether formed an interesting picture of savage manners, in which ferocity was strongly blended with humanity, for their respect and devotion to the old sybil was manifested as feelingly as their hatred towards those whom they call their enemies: in fact, the young warrior chiefs presenting to her (as was the case with several) their first spoils of conquest, reminded me of young lions bringing part of the spoils of the chase to their aged dam.

In this affray only a few of Atoi's party had been wounded, and twenty-five of the enemy had been killed. It was a fortunate circumstance for the wretched prisoners that none of the conquering party had been killed; for, if that had been the case, there would have been a dreadful slaughter of the captives on their arrival at the village, an act of cruelty never dispensed with. This sight I dreaded I should encounter when I went to witness the disembarkation; but, hoping that my presence might be some restraint upon their barbarities, I awaited the result with as much firmness as I was master of.

Old Pa and Whalers at Bay of Islands.

CHAPTER XLIII

VISITS OF WHALERS

Two South Sea whalers were at this time lying in the bay: the Anne, from London, a full ship; and the Lynx, from Sydney. Since I have been living here, five vessels of this description have visited us; and many others would have touched here but for the want of proper regulations, and a dread of the dispositions of the natives. There being here no representatives of the British Government, the crews of whalers are often involved in disputes with the natives. This want of Government support has also frightened other vessels away; their commanders preferring going on to Port Jackson, where they half ruin themselves by the unavoidable expenses they incur. Even when their vessels have anchored here, the thoughtlessness and eccentricity of this class of men, when they are under no restraint or control, has sometimes not only led to disputes with the natives, but with each other, which eventually have proved equally detrimental. In short, New Zealand is a place of such vast importance to so many lucrative branches of British trade, that it must be well worthy the speedy attention of our Government at home.

We spoke frequently to our friend George, as well as to several other of their powerful chiefs, respecting the erection of a small fort with a British garrison, and of permanently hoisting the English flag. They always expressed the utmost delight at the idea; and, from all I have seen of them, I feel convinced it would prove a most politic measure. George (who had visited Port Jackson) said: "This country is finer than Port Jackson; yet the English go and settle there. Our people are much better than the black natives of New South Wales, and yet you English live amongst them in preference to us."

The ship Anne, Captain Gray, was out three years, and during that period she never entered a civilised port. She had touched twice at this bay, and had cruised four months on the coast of Japan, off Timor, through the Sandwich and Friendly Islands, and passed several times over the Pacific Ocean, in order to obtain a cargo of sperm oil, which she at length accomplished; and was at this time here to refit for her voyage home to England round Cape Horn, having picked up most of her cargo off this port.

For twelve years past, notwithstanding all the disadvantages, this has been the favourite resort for ships in the above-mentioned trade. Here, surrounded with savages and cannibals, they heave down their vessels, land the cargoes and stores, and carry on work, both on board and on shore, in tolerable security. The safety of the harbour, the facility of wooding and watering, the supplies of pigs and potatoes, tempt them to run the risk of placing themselves in the power of capricious and barbarous people.

It has been imagined that the residence of missionaries would have the effect of civilising the natives, and adding to the safety of ships touching here; but experience fully proves the fallacy of such an expectation. These people, abstracted by their own gloomy reflections, look with contempt on all who are in the pursuit of "worldly wealth"; and regard the arrival of a whaler as an enemy coming to interfere with the spiritual interests of "their flock," as they term the inhabitants, though I never yet saw one proselyte of their converting.

They never visit a whaler except on a Sunday, and then it is to beg for the benefit of their society. It cannot, therefore, be expected that much sympathy can exist between parties, where the cold formality of one excites the contempt and disgust of the other.

The ship Anne, of which I have formerly spoken, arrived here lately from Wahoo, one of the Sandwich Islands, which possesses the advantage of a British consul. The pacific disposition and orderly government of the natives do not require a British garrison, or any war-like force; and of the excellent effects produced by this representation of our Government Captain Gray speaks with admiration and enthusiasm. The harbours were crowded with shipping; houses, nay, even streets, were beginning to appear; the savage character of the people was gradually subsiding into industrious and peaceful occupations; and comfort and prosperity were spreading their benign influence over the whole island: yet Wahoo is not nearly so well situated as a rendezvous for South Sea whalers as New Zealand; at least so I have been informed by all the captains of those ships who have conversed with me on the subject.

It is rather a remarkable and novel circumstance that the natives, who have been now for fourteen or fifteen years in close intercourse and carrying on traffic with Europeans, should not, in the course of that period, understand the nature and value of money; a laughable instance of which occurred to us a few days since. A native came to our house with a serious countenance and business-like manner, and said he wished to purchase a musket: we asked to see what he had brought in exchange for one, when, with great ceremony, he produced a copper penny piece in the way of payment. The poor fellow had, doubtless, seen some one pass a doubloon, and had mistaken his penny for one; as a doubloon is about the price given for a musket in our regulated list of charges. We, of course, refrained from laughter; but he was quite astonished and mortified when he was made to understand we could not trade with him. He took a stroll round the beach, offering his penny, by way of barter, to every white man he met, but everywhere with equally bad success.

CHAPTER XLIV

VISIT OF TWO SOUTH SEA ISLANDERS

When our brig left Tucopea she brought away two natives of that island, who had most earnestly entreated the captain to take them off, and leave them upon any other land he pleased, as, according to their statement, Tucopea was so overstocked with inhabitants that it was scarcely possible to find subsistence; and the scarcity of food had become so general, that parents destroyed their children rather than witness their sufferings from famine. Captain Kent, therefore, from motives of compassion, received them on board his ship; and, not having touched at any inhabited spot, brought them with him here. Their extraordinary appearance excited a great deal of surprise, both among Europeans and New Zealanders. They appeared simple, timid creatures, though stout and comely, but their hair was unlike anything I had before beheld, as in length it reached below the waist, and was so abundantly thick as completely to conceal their faces. By some curious chemical process which the natives of Tucopea have discovered, they render their hair a bright sulphur colour; and, as this mass of yellow hangs over their faces and shoulders, they bear the most striking resemblance to the lion monkeys of the Brazils.

These poor creatures, upon landing, shook with fear, and trembled greatly when they beheld the New Zealanders, whose character for cannibalism had reached even their remote island: when our friend George went up to them, and lifted up (in order to examine closely) the curious mass of hair in which they were enveloped, they burst into a passionate fit of tears, and ran up to us for protection. The New Zealanders, with characteristic cunning, perceiving the horror they had created, tormented them still more cruelly, by making grotesque signs, as if they were about to commence devouring them; and, at the same time (like most savages), evincing the most sovereign contempt for them, from their apparent pusillanimity.

After they had been some days on shore, we had a very diverting scene with them, which exhibited strongly the great difference there is in the nature of the two classes of savages we now had such opportunities of observing. I had brought my violin from Sydney, on which I used to play occasionally. The New Zealanders generally expressed the greatest dislike to it; and my companions used to rally me much on the subject, saying it was not that the savages did not like music, but it was my discordant playing that frightened them away, which might be true. It was, however, a useful discovery for us all, as I often took that method of civilly driving them out of our house when we grew tired of their company. But when I began to play before the Tucopeans, the effect it had instantly upon them was ludicrous in the extreme. They sprang up, and began dancing most furiously; at the same time, so waving their heads about as to keep their long hair extended at its fullest length: as I played faster, they quickened their pace. A lively Scotch reel seemed to render them nearly frantic; and when I ceased playing, they threw themselves down on the floor quite exhausted, and unable to articulate a word. I have observed (generally speaking) that savages are not much affected by music; but these two Tucopeans were excited to a most extraordinary degree.

CHAPTER XLV

THE DEATH OF HONGI

We at length received authentic intelligence of the death of the celebrated Hongi. Finding his dissolution fast approaching, he convened a meeting of all the neighbouring chiefs; and as many as could reach the spot in time attended. The wounded warrior expired, surrounded by the men he had so frequently led to battle and conquest. After the numerous and desperate risks he had run, the many encounters he had sustained with various enemies, it appeared extraordinary to us Europeans that he should die quietly in his hut. It is the custom to keep a guarded and mysterious silence relating to the subjects which are spoken of by a dying chief. I questioned several who had attended Hongi: all spoke with the greatest solemnity of his last moments. One sentence (uttered by him) was all I could obtain after much manoeuvring, and that was spoken but a few minutes before he breathed his last, which was, that "Shulitea (viz., our friend George) would not live one week longer than himself"; but, as our patron was in perfect health at the time, and all seemed peaceful around him, I only laughed at the improbability of the prophecy being fulfilled.

The natives of New Zealand pay the greatest respect to courage and war-like talents: these were the only distinguishing characteristics of Hongi; yet, by possessing these, he was more feared, and had a greater number of followers, than any other chief in the island. His hereditary possessions were but small, and his name was little known; yet his undaunted courage, his skill, and success in many sanguinary battles, made him, at length, a most powerful chief, and obtained for him that which is considered wealth in this country, namely, an immense number of slaves. In his last moments he was attended by more men of rank than had ever before assembled to witness the dissolution of a warrior, and this is considered the greatest proof of attention and respect one chieftain can show towards another.

CHAPTER XLVI

A TRIBAL CONFLICT

Our brig now sailed for Hokianga to take in a cargo of planks; and my friend, Mr. Shand, being tired of wandering, accompanied her; but I, being still anxious to procure more sketches of this interesting country, determined to remain as long as possible, and to take one more walk across the island, and join the brig by the time she was loaded. I was preparing to start on my last pedestrian tour, when a chain of events occurred which threw all the tribes into confusion. Bloodshed and devastation stared me in the face from all quarters; and from the state of security I had imagined myself to be in, I was roused to behold myself beset with difficulties; to crown which, our brig, which would have been a place of safety and refuge, was now on the opposite side of the island.

Arising from a trifling circumstance, which was partly caused by us, though innocently, Pomare's only son had lost his life; and, as is usual among savage tribes, the severest retaliation soon took place.

By relating the particulars, the reader will perceive how easily the war-cry is raised among these turbulent savages.

Pomare's only surviving son. Tiki, was a very finely-formed, handsome young man, of twenty years of age, and he had made an arrangement with a captain of a ship here to supply him with a certain number of hogs. Accordingly, accompanied by a party of his friends, he started into the interior for the purpose of collecting them. In making his selection, he not only proceeded to drive off some of his own, but actually laid claim to, and began marching away with, some belonging to his neighbours. The right owners remonstrated with him in vain. He, being an insolent, over-bearing young fellow, persisted in his unjust claims, and set them all at defiance. They were compelled to yield up their property, as his tribe was a most powerful one; and Tiki was driving away the stolen hogs in triumph, when a sudden stop was put to his predatory career.

Finding words were of no avail to induce the young man to restore the swine, one of the injured party had recourse to a musket. A bullet, aimed from behind a tree, killed Tiki on the spot; but from whose hand it came could only be conjectured. The greatest confusion instantly took place. His companions, being well armed, the war-cry was immediately raised; and the fray becoming general, seven more lives were lost.

When the account of this melancholy affair reached our beach, everyone flew to arms, even all the women, for the young man was a general favourite. The war-cry spread in every direction. "Here," they exclaimed, "is the last of the Pomare family killed treacherously, a warrior related to and connected with every chief of consequence in the country, and a nephew of the great Shulitea." The cry for blood and revenge was universal. I must confess that, added to the danger it placed me in, I was much shocked when I heard of the fate of poor Tiki, for he was one of our particular friends, and had passed many an evening in our hut. I had taken leave of him only the day before, when he had set out, full of health and spirits, on this hog expedition, which had terminated thus fatally.

The death of this young man excited the highest indignation in the minds of his countrymen, as well as in those of his numerous intimate friends and relations; for a report was industriously circulated that he had fallen by the hands of a slave. This was considered by his tribe as a degradation infinitely worse than the murder itself. The offended chiefs assembled on our beach, with all their followers, armed: and none appeared more indignant at the transaction than our friend George, who, with his brother Kiney Kiney, placed themselves at the head of the party, to revenge the insult which had been offered them.

The night before they started on this expedition, George spent the evening with us. He was in particularly low spirits, and said he did not at all like the business he was going upon: but, as he was the nearest relation of the deceased, and the eldest of the tribe, he went in hopes of being able to prevent a great effusion of blood, and also to restrain the impetuosity of the young men. Little did we then think he would be the first victim; although his unusual depression of mind brought to my remembrance the prophecy of Hongi, and, spite of my endeavours to banish my forebodings, I felt convinced that the prediction would in all probability be fulfilled.

Three days had elapsed from the time the avenging party had gone on their mission, when, at midnight, a messenger, faint and nearly exhausted, arrived on our beach with the following dreadful intelligence; and that night no other sounds were heard than those of agony and woe, the yelling of women, and the shrieks of slaves.

The substance of the man's information was, that George and the offending party had met; but, as several days had passed since the murder of their friend, their feelings were in some degree appeased, and they had contented themselves with a general plunder of whatever property their enemies possessed. They had spared their lives, and the outrage was considered as atoned for. The chiefs were on their return home, laden with spoil, when, like other coalesced armies, disagreements began to take place among themselves, and discord long smothered, broke out in every quarter of the camp.

George, the principal person of their party, was the one marked to be dissatisfied with. All were jealous of him, in consequence of his possessions at Kororarika giving him such a decided advantage over every other tribe, by his trade and intercourse with Europeans. It is probable, also, that as the other tribes went forth with an intention to fight, they were resolved not to be disappointed, and therefore determined to create a feud among themselves, rather than return home devoid of the pleasures or the trophies of a combat.

Some irritating language had been uttered by both sides, when an accident of a fatal nature took place, which produced an instantaneous and general appeal to arms. At the close of the day a halt was made, as usual, and each party began erecting their temporary huts to pass the night in. One of George's wives, assisted by a little boy, his nephew, was busily engaged in constructing one; arms and baggage of every description being strewed about in all directions. At this period a lad took up one of George's muskets, and began to play with it; but not understanding the management of it, he, by his injudicious handling, accidentally discharged the piece, and killed both the wife and nephew, the ball passing through both their bodies.

The sensation produced by this unfortunate accident may readily be conceived. As the woman who was killed was related to the tribe who had been disputing with George all day, her death furnished an ostensible motive for open war; and before the real cause of the accident could be explained, another shot was fired, which wounded a chief of the name of Moo-de-wy in the thigh. This proved the signal for a general fight: each party ran to their arms, ranged themselves under their different leaders, and a general discharge of muskets immediately took place.

Almost at the beginning of the combat George received a shot, which broke both his legs: his brother and friends endeavoured to support him in their arms. It being then nearly dark, added much to the confusion, as it was difficult to distinguish friend from foe; indeed, so sudden had been the onset, that many could scarcely have been aware of the cause of the contest. But our unhappy friend, who seemed particularly marked out in this unfortunate affray, soon after received another bullet, which struck him on the throat, and terminated his existence; thus dying before a week had passed since the death of his rival Hongi. I heard from one of his friends who supported him in his last moments, that he died like a hero: finding both his legs were broken, and that consequently he was totally unable to move, he begged those friends who were about him to leave him to his fate, and either again enter the fight, or make their escape while they yet had time. He then gave his musket to one, took off his mantle to present to another, and while thus in the act of exhorting his friends and distributing amongst them his tokens of regard, he received his death-wound, and expired without a groan. When George fell, a general flight took place; and though the engagement had lasted but a short time, great numbers had fallen on both sides.

CHAPTER XLVII

THE DEATH OF KING GEORGE AND ITS CONSEQUENCES

This news caused mourning and lamentation along our beach, and filled all the Europeans with dismay. We could not calculate the extent of the injury we might receive, but felt certain we should be considerable sufferers in some way or other. The light of day seemed to add to, rather than to diminish, the moans of George's faithful subjects. The violent sobbings from every dwelling were most dismal. Groups were scattered about, forming small crying parties, and cutting their skins deeply with knives and pieces of broken glass; in short, nothing was heard but yelling and groaning, and nothing was seen but streams of blood!

But however shocked I might feel by the train of accidents and deaths which had made such cruel havoc amongst my friends, and notwithstanding my sincere grief and regret for the fate of poor George, who was a most humane and intelligent chief, and particularly kind to all the English; the predicament in which I was now placed demanded all my energies, for I felt that I stood in a situation of great danger.

I have before noticed their barbarous custom, on the death of a chief, of plundering his family and friends. As we had always been considered as a part of George's family, living under his protection, adopted by him, and admitted into his tribe, I entertained great suspicions that we also should be sufferers by the general plunder about to take place: besides, I was so circumstanced as to be obliged to cross the country with all my goods, and my route lay through the territories of all those chiefs who had been fighting against George; and I was at no loss to guess in what light they would regard me. Depending, too securely, on the general tranquility, I had not sent my luggage by sea, as I might have done, and which would have saved me great anxiety, as I should have ventured alone without fear, but could not manage to carry what I possessed; and to engage any to convey them was an impossibility, for the moment I made the proposition to any (even the meanest of the slaves) to accompany me, they ran off into the bush, nor could any entreaty, presents, or threats induce them to venture with me; so, for security, I removed all the property I had, and went with it on board the Marianne, whaler.

For three days after the death of George, all gave themselves up to grief; no work was done, and not an individual was to be seen but in an agony of tears. I began to feel strangely affected with melancholy myself, when, on the fourth morning, a scene of bustle took place, and low spirits were banished by tumult, noise, and confusion.

At six o'clock on that morning we discovered upwards of twenty sail of war canoes, crowded with armed warriors, coming into the bay. What their intentions were we could not imagine; but for fear of the worst, the ships in the harbour shotted their guns, and when the canoes were abreast of us, we fired a blank one over their heads. On this they all stopped, and we saw some stir amongst them: at length a very small canoe left the main body, and pulled directly towards us; it contained the chief persons of the expedition: they came on board, and assured us they meant no harm to any persons; they were merely some of the late George's friends, who were going to pay a visit of condolence to his relations; and, after making a most hearty breakfast with us, they went on shore, and we accompanied them.

Whether the account they gave of themselves was correct, or the reverse, we knew not at the time; but we felt assured their intentions were not hostile towards us Europeans, and their quarrels with each other we were determined not to interfere in. We soon discovered their falsehood, for George's eldest daughter informed me that amongst the chiefs who landed with us were several of the most inveterate foes of her father, and that they were only restrained from committing the most dreadful outrages, and carrying off all her relations as slaves, by witnessing the many friends of George by whom they were surrounded. The day was spent in savage dancing, yelling, making speeches, and debating as to who the proper person was to succeed George in his dignities: several times I thought the affair would end in blows. George's relation, Rivers, made great exertions "to keep the peace," and finally, by force of argument, succeeded. It was at length unanimously agreed that Kiney Kiney was to succeed his brother, and that Rivers should take the command until the time of Kiney Kiney's mourning for the loss of George should be completed.

CHAPTER XLVIII

DEPARTURE FROM BAY OF ISLANDS

After these important matters were amicably disposed of, I made a sign to Rivers, and, separating him from the crowd, I explained to him the nature of my situation, and asked his assistance in getting me safely over to Hokianga. He replied, there would certainly be great danger in attempting it; but I soon discovered that he magnified the difficulties in order to increase his demand for payment, for even the greatest chiefs have here their price. He said (and I had every reason to think he was correct) that I ran no risk of being molested by any chiefs, like himself, who would always protect rather than molest every European; but that the country being in such a state of commotion, in consequence of the late events, it was full of runaway slaves, who always took advantage of such times to make their escape; and if I chanced to fall in with any of them, I should be exposed to great peril: "However (he added), keep up your spirits; I have two confidential slaves, who shall conduct you over, and carry your luggage, if you will make me a present of a stocking full of powder, a bag of small shot, and a powder-horn." He also proposed, as he himself was going to the Kirikiri, and thence to a village in the interior, to meet a large assemblage of chiefs, in order to talk over the late tragical events, that I should journey the first part of my way with him, in his own canoe.

Accordingly, after having made preparations for my departure, I took leave of all my friends at the Bay of Islands, both civilised and savage. I must say I felt considerable regret when I found myself really going to take final leave of several native families, with whom I had been on terms of intimacy since my residence here, from whom I had received many proofs of personal regard, and whom, I felt convinced, I should never meet or hear of more; none I regretted parting with more than the family of poor Shulitea; the mere sight of me seemed to rekindle all their grief for the loss of their kinsman, and to remind them more forcibly than ever of his tragical fate. His mother, old Turero, in point of grief, had rivalled Niobe; she had never ceased weeping and lamenting from the time she heard of her son's death, and had twice attempted to strangle herself. But even in the midst of her passionate sorrow, I could scarcely refrain from laughing, while observing her care and anxiety to get all she could from me. After deploring the sad fate of her dear son, "You know," she continued, "you promised him that you would send him a handsome new musket from Sydney; and now, poor fellow, he is dead; and cannot shoot with it; but then you must remember that his brother Kiney Kiney is still alive, and he can shoot with it; and poor George would wish that his brother should have his new musket." This speech I felt quite irresistible; therefore, in order to comfort the old queen, I promised that I would send the musket for her second son; which declaration seemed to afford her great consolation, and considerably abated the violence of her grief.

Just at the dawn of morning we started from the bay in Rivers' canoe, accompanied by his wife, one child, and the two stout slaves he had mentioned to me. My luggage, which consisted of one leathern portmanteau and my bed, was placed in the centre. I had also provided myself with a small basket of cooked meat, with bread, and a small bottle of brandy, which was given me by the captain of one of the whalers. The day broke around us with more than usual brightness; the dewy mists of night were just rising from the waters, and the huge and abrupt forms of the mountains were beginning to develop themselves; flights of wild ducks and stray birds skimmed rapidly by us. The thoughts that crowded my mind were strange and varied, while contemplating scenes of such tranquil beauty as were now presented, glowing with the tints of the rising sun. I contrasted these with the difficulties and dangers I might have to encounter from hordes of ferocious savages, who, now flushed with conquest, were plotting murder and destruction against each other: even a glance at my companions banished all peaceful illusions. While the wife, son, and slaves were using the paddles with the greatest exertions, Rivers was carefully examining his weapons. The beauty of the morning and the romantic scenery was unnoticed: his thoughts were directed solely to contemplating the depth and the width of my stocking of powder, which seemed to afford him infinite satisfaction. He had with him a beautiful double-barrelled gun, and a very good Tower musket; and seeing so many wild ducks fly past, he drew the bullet out of one of the barrels of the former, and, with some of my stock of small shot, fired occasionally amongst them.

At about eight o'clock a light sea breeze sprang up: they then set their sail, and all went to sleep, excepting one slave, who was employed to steer the canoe; so that I had ample time to ruminate upon my solitary and perilous situation. The tide failed us at twelve o'clock, and we then went on shore, kindled a fire, and soon collected such a supply of shell-fish as furnished us a splendid repast. Here we remained till the flood-tide set in strong, when, again hoisting our sail, we arrived at the Kirikiri about sunset.

I here found the missionaries in the greatest consternation and dismay, and learned that it was one of the chiefs of Hokianga who had shot George, and they dreaded lest the result of that deed should be that the whole of the savage tribes on that part of the island would be opposed to each other; that combats would ensue; and which side soever might be victorious, it would prove equally injurious to them, as they had settlements on both sides of the island. But their greatest alarm was occasioned by their possessions at Hokianga, as the most violent depredations were there being committed; and as this was the very point of my destination, the news was not very consolatory to me. "So anxious," said one of "the brethren" to me, "were we to inform our Christian brethren of our danger, that we actually gave a *warm piece* to a native to carry a letter over to you, although that is strictly contrary to our orders." I expressed a desire to know what he meant by a *warm piece*; he kicked his foot against the stock of a gun I had at the time in my hand; and, looking at me with an expression of the greatest contempt, said, "It is what *you worldly* folks call a musket!"

They were making considerable preparations to repair to the great meeting of the chiefs, to which Rivers was journeying. This was a wise and politic measure for them to pursue; and they were highly delighted to have such an addition to their party as this well-known chief; and though they would not acknowledge it, their satisfaction was very visible. I earnestly requested them to inform me candidly, from all they had heard, whether they thought I might, with safety, venture across the country; but I could get nothing from them but vague and mysterious answers: one thing, however, they made me very clearly understand; which was, that they neither cared for me nor for my drawings; that their own safety engrossed all their thoughts; and that a worldly-minded, misguided creature like me was but as dust in the balance, compared to such godly people as themselves, who were now placed in jeopardy. They, without scruple, applied quotations from the Scriptures to themselves, such as, "Why do the heathen so furiously rage," etc., etc.

My necessities compelled me to request a favour from them, which was, that they would allow one of their boys, who could speak English, to accompany me, as our loads were heavy; and his being known to belong to their establishment I thought might be some protection; but the short answer of the monosyllable "*No*" soon made me repent having asked it. I spread my bed in one of their empty rooms; and started at daybreak next morning, with my two native slaves. I could not banish from my remembrance the inhospitable conduct of these missionaries; they never even inquired whether I had any provision for a journey they themselves would not have dared to undertake, which was evident by their giving a native a *warm piece* for merely taking a letter for them. As my shoes were nearly worn out, and I had a long distance to go, over execrable roads, I had intended asking them for a new pair, as they had abundance of everything of the kind sent to them from England, to distribute to the needy (and I fully came under that description of character); but finding them so selfish and cold-hearted, and meeting with one refusal, I refrained, and set off, literally almost barefooted.

CHAPTER XLIX

THE JOURNEY TO HOKIANGA

We journeyed on all day by a road I had never been before, my attendants evidently taking by-paths to avoid meeting stragglers or runaways. I was well laden, having to carry my musket and my basket of provisions; and each of my men, in addition to the loads I had placed on his shoulders, bore a basket of potatoes. Once or twice, during our route, we saw some persons at a distance, and I was sorry to notice the great alarm it occasioned to my companions, as I now had every reason to apprehend, that, in case of danger, they would slip off their burdens, make their escape, and leave me and my baggage to my fate, which the missionaries had told me they considered a thing very likely to happen. Once we heard a great firing of muskets, which I afterwards ascertained to be the *feu de joie* fired at the first meeting of the chiefs, at their grand assembling in the neutral village.

At night, we arrived safe at Patuone's Village, where I had slept on my first journey across the island; but it now presented a very different appearance to what it had done then; instead of the tumult I had formerly heard, all was silence; the numerous families then there, all fully occupied, were exchanged for a few old surly-looking slaves, and the huts were all deserted. The inhabitants, in consequence of the rumour of approaching war, having betaken themselves to one of their fortified pas, I had no alternative but to pass the night with these suspicious-looking creatures, who, feeling themselves beyond the control of their cruel masters, soon gave way to their own vile passions, and became most impertinent and intrusive—taking every advantage of my loneliness to indulge their curiosity and familiarity.

On my arrival, I had deposited my things in one of the empty huts, and spread my bed, hoping to enjoy the luxury of a few hours' repose after the fatigue and great anxieties of the day; but these fellows would force themselves into the hut I had chosen, where they lighted a fire, and sat chattering around it all the night long. Finding that I did not appear alarmed at their intrusion or noise, they kept doing everything they could think of to rouse my fears. They threatened to break open my portmanteau; and one old wretch sharpened his knife, and made motions as though he were going to cut my throat and eat me. I knew my only chance of safety was not to betray any sign of apprehension; so I forced a laugh, and made them believe I considered their tricks an excellent joke. I gave them all my tobacco to keep them in good humour; but I passed a most miserable night, nearly suffocated with smoke, distracted with their noise, and annoyed by vermin of every description.

I was most happy when daybreak gave me an excuse for leaving these brutal savages, and resuming my journey. Every step I took brought before me proofs of the horrors of war: villages which had been crowded, were now entirely desolate, and, in many instances, burned to the ground. On that spot where I had left a party of enterprising Scotchmen busily employed in sawing timber, with crowds of natives assisting them, all was quiet and totally deserted, with the exception of a few nearly starved, wretched-looking dogs, who, hearing someone approach, came out, and tried to bark at us, but were too weak to utter a sound.

CHAPTER L

EUROPEAN PREPARATIONS FOR DEFENCE

Our march along the banks of the river was through a most beautiful country; but all the inhabitants had fled; their plantations were in a most luxuriant state; fields which I had left bare and uncultivated were now covered with Indian corn standing higher than my head, the ripe ears hanging fantastically in all directions, and none to gather in the harvest; the crops of kumara and potatoes were equally abundant. I could not help thinking that, if they expected an invasion of their enemies, they had left an ample supply of forage for their use. In the evening I arrived at Horeke, or Deptford Dock-yard (of which I made mention in my first journey). I here found my countrymen in a state of considerable embarrassment. The various chiefs of that district had encamped all round them; so near to them had they taken up their position, that, whatever might be the result of their battles, the European settlement would be in danger. The settlers had fortified their place of refuge in the best manner they could; and all were determined to defend themselves and property to the last. They had four nine-pounders mounted on a hill, and a tolerable battery made of three-inch pine stuff.

Before the English erected their fortifications, there was a great difference of opinion amongst them as to the propriety and utility of adopting so strong a measure, and the affair was finally put to the vote, when the majority proved to be in favour of a strong resistance. I opposed the measure all I could, for I felt convinced that in the event of our allies being worsted we all should be involved in one common massacre; whereas, if no resistance was made, plunder alone would have been the extent of the injury we should suffer; and even of that taking place I had strong doubts. However, as my opinion was overruled, I had to submit, which I did unhesitatingly; and, like a good soldier, I held myself in readiness in case of an attack.

The proprietor and manager of the Dock-yard possessed certainly a "satisfying reason" for striving to defend himself at all hazards. The vessel I had left here, on my former visit, in frame, was now nearly completed, and a most beautiful one she was. He told me he would much rather part with life than see her destroyed; and I confess I could fully enter into his feelings on the subject; but as I had no such object at stake, and was not quite enthusiastic enough to fight for a vessel I had no share in, I felt very much inclined to let the natives war among themselves without interference; but as we Europeans had agreed to assist each other, I would not be behind-hand.

I discharged Rivers' two slaves, and rewarded them liberally for conducting me with safety through such a wild and perilous country; they departed (after expressing the heartiest wishes for my reaching my own home in safety, and thanks for my generosity) to join their master at the great meeting of the chiefs in the interior. These men, while assisting me, were performing a great service to their master, by acting as spies. When we started from the Kirikiri each was armed with a musket; but when we had accomplished about half the journey, they concealed these in a hollow tree, under pretence of extreme fatigue. I felt convinced at the time that was not their real reason for so doing; and afterwards I learned the true motive. Had they been found armed when returning to their master (who was hostile to those assembled round the Dock-yard), they would have been detained; but, by their coming unarmed amongst us, they were suffered to depart; and I have no doubt the information they carried back to Rivers was very important. I did not mention to anyone the hiding of these muskets in the woods, though, according to "The Articles of War," I ought to have done so, as getting possession of them would have added two more to our strength, and lessened that of our enemy; my silence arose from a repugnance I felt to betray these poor creatures, who had behaved so well to me.

Although prepared for war, we were very well pleased to find no attack was made upon us. Indeed, from the first, it had been my decided opinion, that unless we interfered, and made ourselves by that means obnoxious, they had too much respect for us, and were too anxious to retain our kindly feelings towards them, to molest us;

at the same time, I felt that it might be a very politic measure to show them what powerful resistance we could make, if driven to extremities.

After passing a week of the greatest anxiety, on account of our expected invasion, it afforded us the utmost satisfaction to receive a visit from Mr. Hobbs, the Wesleyan missionary, one of the persons who had visited the war-camp of the assembled chiefs, who were convened, on the death of our lamented friend George, to debate and decide upon the momentous question of peace or war.

The subject (our informant stated) had been gone into at great length, and stormy and fierce had been the discussion. Finally, the good sense of the elder and more experienced chiefs prevailed over the fiercer passions of the younger, and peace was decided upon. This event forms a new era in "The Political History of the Few Zealanders," it being the first time so great an assemblage had met to discuss openly a national question, or in which they had allowed cool reasoning and good sense to prevail over their habitual ferocity. As may naturally be supposed, where such various interests were at stake, this pacific measure was not effected without considerable opposition from the young and furious chiefs. The provocations given by them to the elders, whose voices were for peace, were considerable. They did not confine themselves to abuse, but fired several muskets during debate, in hopes that one shot out of the many might prove fatal; which, if it had, and any distinguished chief had been killed, or even wounded, it would have immediately thrown all into confusion. Even when pacific measures were decided upon by a very large majority, and the chiefs were about to separate, a bullet was fired from the pa, which had evidently been aimed at a chief, a well-known ally of the late Shulitea, as it fell at his feet, and the earth it threw up fell upon him. For a few seconds surprise kept all silent; but, as the angry chief rose up, and was about to address the crowd, his friends eagerly surrounded him, and hurried him away.

This was the first instance on record, in which these people had laid a statement of their private wrongs before a public assembly consisting of deputies from every part of the island, and abided by the decision of the majority; and it was the only instance of a chief being killed in battle, and his decease not having been followed up by the plundering and destruction of his whole family or tribe.

This had been a question of peculiar interest to us Europeans, as several of their great men had fallen in a skirmish (whether an accidental one or a decided combat made not the slightest difference). We knew their barbarous custom; and, consequently, we were preparing for scenes of deadly revenge and insatiable fury to be acted by both parties, and which must have involved all settled here in destruction. Our feelings may therefore be imagined, when we were informed that a parliament had been convened, and all the parties interested were present by invitation, and took part in the debate. A central spot was fixed on to accommodate the various chieftains. The causes of the accident were then explained; they wept and lamented the fallen chiefs, and finally retired satisfied to their several homes. Surely everyone who is interested in tracing our own form of government, from the present time up to its first rude outline, will perceive the similarity of causes and events, and will anticipate the glorious prospect of beholding a clever, brave, and, I may add, noble race of men, like the New Zealanders, rescued from barbarism. This pacific and rational discussion among the chiefs seems, in reality, to give promise of the germ of a regular reform. Should a few more such meetings take place, and terminate in the same amicable manner (and I think it very probable), some clever individual may rise up amongst them, take the reins in his own hands, and establish something like a regular form of government.

CHAPTER LI

OBSERVATIONS ON THE SOCIAL CONDITIONS OF THE
MAORIS

Feeling that I was not likely now to be called upon to act offensively, I considered myself at liberty to make numerous excursions round our fortress, not only to admire this fertile and beautiful country, but to visit some of my old friends. I was very much astonished and shocked at seeing several very beautiful young women, whom I left only a few months back in perfect health and strength, now reduced to mere "living skeletons," and also to hear of the death of others by consumption. This disease seems to be the scourge of the young; and when they are once seized with its symptoms, they are very speedily brought to the grave. The natives say, "It is Atua, the Great Spirit, coming into them, and eating up their inside; for the patient can feel those parts gradually go away, and then they become weaker and weaker till no more is left; after which the Spirit sends them to the happy island." They never attempt any means of curing or of alleviating the pains caused by this cruel complaint; and all those under its influence are tabooed. I procured from the brig all my remaining stores of tapioca, sago, arrowroot, and sugar, and distributed them in the best way I could amongst my sick friends. They were anxious for wine; but that portion of my sea-stock, as well as spirits, had been long since expended.

It seems unaccountable that the natives of an atmosphere so dry as this is—a country in which there are no marshy bogs, and where, though there is an abundance of water, it is generally seen in clear and sparkling rills rushing down from the mountains into the rivers—should be subject to so fatal a disease as galloping consumption. The only cause to which I can attribute such an affliction is, their indifference to lying out all night exposed to every change of weather—to cold and rain—which, in young and tender constitutions, must produce the most pernicious consequences. If some few are rendered hardy and robust by this process, many, no doubt, are killed by it. I endeavoured to impress on the minds of all my female friends the great danger of thus exposing themselves to cold; but they only laughed at my precautions, and said, "If Atua wished it, so it must be; they could not strive with the Great Spirit."

I have heard so much said about the great impropriety of the white settlers admitting the native females into their society, so much of the scandalous conduct of captains of ships suffering their men to have sweethearts during their stay in port, and so much urged in justification of the indignation shown by the missionaries when this subject is touched on by them, that I feel it necessary to state one decided benefit which has resulted from that intercourse, and which, in my opinion, far more than counterbalances the evil against which there has been raised so loud an outcry.

Before our intercourse took place with the New Zealanders, a universal and unnatural custom existed amongst them, which was that of destroying most of their female children in infancy, their excuse being that they were quite as much trouble to rear, and consumed just as much food, as a male child, and yet, when grown up, they were not fit to go to war as their boys were. The strength and pride of a chief then consisted in the number of his sons; while the few females who had been suffered to live were invariably looked down upon by all with the utmost contempt. They led a life of misery and degradation. The difference now is most remarkable. The natives, seeing with what admiration strangers beheld their fine young women, and what handsome presents were made to them, by which their families were benefited, feeling also that their influence was so powerful over the white men, have been latterly as anxious to cherish and protect their infant girls as they were formerly cruelly bent on destroying them. Therefore, if one sin has been, to a certain degree, encouraged, a much greater one has been annihilated. Infanticide, the former curse of this country, and the cause of its scanty population, a crime every way calculated to make men bloody-minded and ferocious, and to stifle every benevolent and tender feeling, has totally disappeared wherever an intercourse has taken place between the natives and the crews of European vessels.

The New Zealand method of "courtship and matrimony" is a most extraordinary one; so much so, that an observer could never imagine any affection existed between the parties. A man sees a woman whom he fancies he should like for a wife; he asks the consent of her father, or, if an orphan, of her nearest relation, which, if he obtains, he carries his "intended" off by force, she resisting with all her strength; and, as the New Zealand girls are generally pretty robust, sometimes a dreadful struggle takes place; both are soon stripped to the skin, and it is sometimes the work of hours to remove the fair prize a hundred yards. If she breaks away, she instantly flies from her antagonist, and he has his labour to commence again. We may suppose that if the lady feels any wish to be united to her would-be spouse, she will not make too violent an opposition; but it sometimes happens that she secures her retreat into her father's house, and the lover loses all chance of ever obtaining her; whereas, if he can manage to carry her in triumph into his own, she immediately, becomes his wife. The women have a decided aversion to marriage, which can scarcely be wondered at, when we consider how they are circumstanced. While they remain single, they enjoy all the privileges of the other sex; they may rove where they please, and bestow their favours on whom they choose, and are entirely beyond control or restraint; but when married their freedom is at an end; they become mere slaves, and sink gradually into domestic drudges to those who have the power of life and death over them; and whether their conduct be criminal or exemplary, they are equally likely to receive a blow, in a moment of passion, of sufficient force to end life and slavery together! There are many exceptions to this frightful picture; and I saw several old couples, who had been united in youth, who had always lived in happiness together, and whose kind and friendly manner towards each other set an example well worthy of imitation in many English families.

CHAPTER LII

A MAORI TANGI

April 2nd.—This day, perceiving that an unusual number of canoes were passing up the river, all proceeding towards the village of Par-Finneigh, we hailed one; and, upon its coming alongside, we inquired what had occurred, for every appearance of bustle or commotion amongst this restless and war-like people is truly alarming. They informed us that the great chief A-Rowa, who died four months since, and the ceremony of whose "lying in state" I had been permitted by his eldest son to be a witness of, was this day to be exposed to the view of his friends; was to be cried over; and was finally to be deposited in the tomb of his ancestors. As this was one of their imposing spectacles which I had never yet seen, I was anxious to witness it. We soon got a boat ready, and a party of us joined the throng, and proceeded with them to the village. Upon our arrival thither, we found an immense concourse of people assembled; for here, as in most uncivilised or early states of society, the disposition and good qualities of the deceased are made known by the number of friends and followers who meet at his funeral. As these New Zealanders were all fully equipped in arms, they had more the appearance of a hostile meeting in an enemy's camp, than of a group of mourners about to be occupied in the melancholy duty of depositing out of sight for ever the last remains of a beloved chief.

Mooetara, the son and successor of the deceased, came to meet us on the beach, and seemed much gratified by our attention, our appearance on this solemn occasion giving him importance in the eyes of all the natives then assembled. He gave orders for our being conducted with much ceremony to the place of mourning, where, amidst a number of uncouth pieces of carving (which, we were informed were all tombs reared in honour of the memory of several former chiefs, and all tabooed), was erected a small hut, covered in at the top with thatch, but open at the sides. In the centre of this hut the bones of the deceased chief were exposed to view. After having undergone the process of decomposition during four months' exposure to heat, wind, and rain, they had been collected, cleaned, and decorated with a quantity of fresh white feathers, which rendered the appearance of the skull still more frightful.

The women here invariably perform the parts of chief mourners; a group of them, with the widow of the deceased at their head, kept up a most mournful cadence, and at every pause in their dismal song slashed their skins with a piece of shell, till their faces, necks, and arms were literally streaming down with blood. This mourning and cutting is completely a matter of business, and is sometimes carried on without their feeling any real sorrow or sympathy. Parties kept arriving, and when there was not room for them to thrust themselves round the hut, they sat down in groups, perfectly unconcerned, employing themselves in cleaning their firelocks, or playing off upon each other some practical joke; but the moment a vacant space was presented near the hut, they deliberately stripped themselves, put on a most sorrowful countenance, and, seating themselves as near to the ornamented bones as possible, they immediately began their howling and slashing; no one seemed to like the idea of being outdone by his neighbour; but when the time allotted to this ceremony had expired, all instantly jumped up, wiped themselves, put on their mats, and joined the busy throng. There was, indeed, one real mourner, who never moved from the bones, nor once lifted up her eyes from them; she neither howled nor cut herself, and yet she inspired me with pity and commiseration for her forlorn state. This woman had been the only wife of the late chief; and I was informed they had lived many years together, and had a large family; she looked as if she herself was on the very brink of the grave. The contemplation of the mouldering remains of her partner through life must have been, even to her savage mind, most lacerating.

After witnessing several parties perform their funeral ceremonies, and imbibing, in some degree, the melancholy tone of mind such a sight must necessarily create, we arose and joined Mooetara. Here I witnessed a scene that reminded me of an English country fair. An immense number of temporary huts had been erected for the accommodation of the chiefs and their families, where they might repose after their exertions, while their slaves cooked their provisions, of which an abundant quantity had been provided, consisting of piles of kumara and Indian corn, with heaps of fish, which were served out, to all who came for them, with a most liberal hand, and which, of course, added not a little to the pleasure of the day. After all had satisfied their hunger (and even the lowest slaves were permitted, on this occasion, to have as much as they wished for) they jumped up, flew to their muskets, and commenced their war dance with great noise and vigour. The violence of their exertions caused their recent wounds to bleed afresh, and added much to the horror of their hideous grimaces. They then divided into two parties, and had a sham battle. I must here do justice to the temperate habits of my savage friends. During my residence in New Zealand, I have known but very few who were addicted to drinking, and I scarcely ever saw one of them in a state of intoxication; and, on this occasion, where a profusion of what they esteem delicacies was provided gratuitously, they partook so moderately of the tempting fare as not to be prevented using the most violent exertions immediately after their meal. The entertainment being now over, the different parties gathered up what remained of the portions of food distributed to them, and without taking any leave of their entertainer, or returning any thanks for his bountiful providing, they all entered their canoes and paddled away.

CHAPTER LIII

CHARACTER OF THE NEW ZEALANDERS

An unfortunate prejudice has gone forth into the world against the natives of New Zealand, which I have always endeavoured to counteract from a sense of justice, and, from a careful review of those circumstances which have fallen immediately under my own observation; this prejudice has long retarded our knowledge of their true character, but error must gradually give way to truth; and as the circumstances which first brought the stigma upon their name come to light, and are investigated and properly explained, I feel confident the conduct of these islanders will be found superior to that of any other nation in the South Seas. If we take the whole catalogue of dreadful massacres they have been charged with, and (setting aside partiality for our own countrymen) allow them to be carefully examined, it will be found that we have invariably been the aggressors; and when we have given serious cause of offence, can we be so irrational as to express astonishment that a savage should seek revenge? The last massacre was that of "The Boyd's" crew; every impartial person who reads the account of that melancholy transaction must acknowledge the unfortunate captain was most to blame. But that event took place nineteen years back; since which time they know us better, and respect us more; in proof of which, four years since, The Mercury brig was taken possession of by a crowd of natives, after they had endured a series of offences and every kind of ill-treatment; but the difference in their fate, compared with that of The Boyd's ship's company, was remarkable, and proved that the savage temper of the natives was much softened down and humanised, as they merely plundered the vessel, but made no attempt to murder or molest any of the crew, who, if they had possessed sufficient courage, would not have sacrificed their vessel; but, being terrified, they abandoned her, and she was finally wrecked. During my residence, I never heard of one of the men having been murdered; and I feel fully convinced no massacres will ever again be committed in any of the ports in New Zealand where European vessels have been accustomed to anchor.

I once saw, with indignation, a chief absolutely knocked overboard from a whaler's deck by the mate. Twenty years ago so gross an insult would have cost the lives of every individual on board the vessel, but, at the time this occurred, it was only made the subject of complaint, and finally became a cause of just remonstrance with the commander of the whaler. The natives themselves (and I have heard the opinions of various tribes) have invariably told me that these things occurred from our want of knowledge of their laws and customs, which compelled them to seek revenge. "It was," they said, "no act of treachery on our part; we did not invite you to our shores for the purpose of plunder and murder: but you came, and ill-used us; you broke into our tabooed grounds. And did not Atua give those bad white men into the hands of our fathers?"

I am confident that a body of Europeans may now reside in perfect security in any part of these islands. The late plundering of the missionaries at Whangaroa was a peculiar circumstance, which might have happened even in civilised Europe, had the seat of war approached so near their place of residence. If their houses and chapel had been on the plains of Waterloo during the June of 1815 they would not have experienced a better fate.

This recent tumult has brought a circumstance into notice highly interesting to all who may hereafter wish to settle here. It has hitherto been their custom, when an accident occurs, such as the sudden death of a chief, to make a general plunder of everything belonging to the family of the deceased, and all under their protection. A knowledge of this horrible custom has deterred many from settling in New Zealand; and even those who have resolved to run so great a risk have lived in a continued state of alarm, lest the death of their protecting chief should leave them at the mercy of a savage enemy.

The deaths of Hongi and Shulitea placed the missionaries and all the settlers on Kororarika Beach in considerable jeopardy: but it appeared as if reason had begun to dawn on the minds of these benighted savages, for this unjust and cruel custom was now for the first time discontinued. I was on the beach at the time when an immense party, well armed, came for the express purpose of satiating their revengeful feelings. I had taken the precaution of removing what I possessed on board a whaler then lying in the harbour. The chiefs first sat down to discuss the matter over amongst themselves, and their deliberations ended in their being satisfied with destroying the village of Matowe, the one adjoining ours, and which had been the residence of Pomare's son, whose death was the cause of all the late turbulent events.

The great and leading defect in this country, and the principal cause of their frequent wars and disturbances, which harass and depopulate the tribes, and puts a stop to all improvement, is the want of some regular system of government. There are only two classes of people—chiefs and slaves; and, as consanguinity constitutes a high claim, the eldest son of a large family, who can bring the greatest number of warriors of his own name into the field, is considered the chief of that district or tribe; and as he, by reason of his followers, can take possession of the greatest number of prisoners or slaves, he becomes the ruling man. Every other man of his tribe considers himself on an equality with him in everything, except that he shows him obedience, and follows him to battle.

Each is independent in his own family, and holds uncontrolled power of life and death over every individual it contains. They seem not to exercise any coercion over the younger branches of a family, who are allowed unbounded liberty till the girls have sweethearts and the boys are strong enough to go to war. They are kind and hospitable to strangers, and are excessively fond of their children. On a journey, it is more usual to see the father carrying his infant than the mother; and all the little offices of a nurse are performed by him with the tenderest care and good humour. In many instances (wherein they differ from most savage tribes) I have seen the wife treated as an equal and companion. In fact, when not engaged in war, the New Zealander is quite a domestic, cheerful, harmless character; but once rouse his anger, or turn him into ridicule, and his disposition is instantly changed. A being, whose passions have never been curbed from infancy, and whose only notion of what he conceives to be his right is to retaliate for an offence with blood, must naturally form a cruel and vindictive character. Such these islanders seemed to us on our first visiting them. The sight of beings so extraordinary (for thus we Europeans must have appeared to them) excited in their savage minds the greatest wonder; and they thought we were sent as a scourge and an enemy; and though Cook, one of their earliest visitors, adopted every method his ingenuity could devise to conciliate them, yet, as they never could thoroughly understand his intentions, they were always on the alert to attack him. Hence arose the horror and disgust expressed formerly at the mere mention of the name of "a New Zealander."

I have often tried, in vain, to account for there being such a decided dissimilarity between the natives of New Holland and New Zealand. So trifling is the difference in their situation on the globe, and so *similar their climates*—both having remained so long unknown to the great continents, and so devoid of intercourse with the rest of the world—that one would be led to imagine a great resemblance must be the result. But the natives of the former seem of the lowest grade—the last link in the great chain of existence which unites man with the monkey. Their limbs are long, thin, and flat, with large bony knees and elbows, a projecting forehead, and pot-belly. The mind, too, seems adapted to this mean configuration; they have neither energy, enterprise, nor industry; and their curiosity can scarcely be excited. A few exceptions may be met with; but these are their general characteristics. While the natives of the latter island are "cast in beauty's perfect mould;" the children are so fine and powerfully made, that each might serve as a model for a statue of "the Infant Hercules;" nothing can exceed the graceful and athletic forms of the men, or the rounded limbs of their young women. These possess eyes beautiful and eloquent, and a profusion of long, silky, curling hair; while the intellects of both sexes seem of a superior order; all appear eager for improvement, full of energy, and indefatigably industrious, and possessing amongst themselves several arts which are totally unknown to their neighbours.

CHAPTER LIV

THE SETTLEMENT AND TRADE OF HOKIANGA

On April the 14th, our brig being stored with planks, flax, and potatoes, and ready for sea, I went on board of her. We had fine weather till we dropped down to the entrance of the river, where we intended taking in our stock of water for the voyage, when the scene suddenly changed, and a severe gale came on, right out to sea, which we could not avail ourselves of; neither could we get the water off, as our rafts of casks got adrift in the attempt to get them on board. To add to our disasters, one of our cables parted, and we had to ride out the gale (of two days' continuance) with one only, the sea rolling heavily right open before us, and we in momentary expectation of the remaining cable's going; we had not a single day's allowance of water on board, and at one period all hands (except the carpenter and passengers) were out of the brig, on shore, filling the casks. Fortunately for us, the cable proved a tough one; had it parted, we should have been in a most perilous situation.

April 20th.—For the last week we were stationary at the river's mouth, waiting for a fair wind to carry us over the bar; and during that time there was no appearance of any change; we also heard that vessels had been detained here for six weeks before they could accomplish it. We were visited daily by parties of natives, who seemed to rejoice at our being delayed, as it gave them more of our company than they had calculated upon. They were more delighted with our society than we were with theirs; in a small vessel they are a serious nuisance, on account of the swarms of vermin they bring with them, and which they communicate liberally to all. Myself and all the passengers on board had our leisure time fully occupied in dislodging these "little familiars" from their strongholds in different parts of our apparel.

During the time we were lying here, I saw and conversed with several individuals who had attended the "Great Meeting," and their accounts gave rise to various opinions respecting the policy of supplying the natives with firearms. As I had always been an advocate for the measure, I was gratified by hearing that it was thought to be in consequence of each party's being possessed of a nearly equal quantity of muskets, that a general and exterminating war was avoided. Some may suppose that similar tranquility would have been preserved, had they been equally well supplied with their native weapons of war; but that would not have been the case. When they found that each party could furnish forth the same number of European muskets, they paused, well knowing that it was contrary to the wish of all the white settlers that they should proceed to hostilities. Indeed, Europeans intrepidly mingled amongst them, urging them to a reconciliation, and threatening that, if they failed in their endeavours, the supplies of arms and ammunition should be discontinued. This threat had its desired effect on the minds of the natives; no blood was spilt, and each chief returned quietly to his own home.

On the night we heard of the death of George and his wife, "Revenge and war" was the universal cry. His party would not believe that it could be an accident, nor would they hear of any apology being received. At this time they imagined the tribes of Hokianga were possessed of but very few firearms; and, as the skirmish took place in that district, it was determined that an exterminating war should be carried into the heart of it. However, before all the preparations could be made to carry their intentions into effect, they received certain information that the people of Hokianga were even better supplied with muskets than those of the Bay of Islands. This intelligence occasioned an assemblage of the different tribes to be proposed, and when it took place the friends of George saw their opponents so well prepared for the "tug of war" that they deemed it judicious to come forward and to shake hands and to acknowledge that the death of Shulitea proceeded either from accident or mistake. A curious circumstance took place in the midst of their debate. An old chief, who wished for a fight, and did not approve of the introduction of firearms, but was an advocate for the old method of New Zealand warfare, proposed that each party should send away *all* their muskets and ammunition, and engage manfully with their own native weapons, and then it could be easily proved which were the "best men;" but this mode of settling the dispute, not being agreeable to the majority, was instantly negatived, and treated with disdain.

The colony of Scotch carpenters, who had formed a settlement at the head of the river, and of whom I made "honourable mention" on my first journey, finding themselves so close to what they feared might become the seat of war, and having no means whatever of defending themselves, made an arrangement with Mooetara, the chief of Parkunugh (which is situated at the entrance of the same river), and placed themselves under his protection. They accordingly moved down here, which gave great satisfaction to that chief. Neither could their former protector, Patuone, feel offended at their removal, from the peculiar nature of the circumstances they were placed in. These hardy North Britons were delighted to find a reasonable excuse for moving, their former establishment being situated too far from the sea for them to reap any advantage from ships coming into port. Nothing can be more gratifying than to behold the great anxiety of the natives to induce Englishmen to settle amongst them; it ensures their safety; and no one act of treachery is on record of their having practised towards those whom they had invited to reside with them.

Mooetara is a man of great property and high rank, and is considered a very proud chief by the natives; yet he is to be seen every day working as hard as any slave in assisting in the erection of houses for the accommodation of his new settlers. He has actually removed from his old village of Parkunugh (a strong and beautiful place), and is erecting huts for his tribe near the spot chosen by his new friends; so that, in a very short time, a barren point of land, hitherto without a vestige of a human habitation, will become a thriving and populous village, for it is incredible how quickly the orders of these chiefs are carried into effect. I was frequently a witness to the short space of time they took to erect their houses; and, though small, they are tight, weather-proof, and warm: their storehouses are put together in the most substantial and workmanlike manner.

It is very difficult to make the New Zealanders explain the nature of their religious belief. One superstition seems general with all the tribes respecting the formation of the world, or, rather, of their own island, for that is the place of the first importance in their estimation. They say a man, or a god, or some great spirit, was fishing in his war-canoe, and pulled up a large fish, which instantly turned into an island; and a lizard came upon that, and brought up a man out of the water by his long hair; and he was the father of all the New Zealanders. Almost all their grotesque carvings are illustrations of this idea in some way or other. The favourite theme on which (I observed) the missionaries discoursed to them were "the torments of hell." This has become a subject of ridicule to most of the natives; they do not deny that there may be such a place, but they add, it is not for them, for if Atua had intended it so he would have sent them word about it long before he sent the white men into their country; and they conclude by stating that they know perfectly well the situation of the island where they are to go to after this life.

CHAPTER LV

MASSACRE OF A SCHOONER'S CREW

While remaining here wind-bound, in imaginary security, and amusing ourselves with noticing the curious customs and peculiarities of these islanders, a dreadful tragedy was taking place only a few miles' distance from us, and to which I before alluded, when I mentioned crossing the bar on our first arrival from Port Jackson. The Enterprise schooner, a very fine vessel, which was built at the settlement on this river, had been sent to Sydney, and while we were lying there we were in hourly expectation of her return. She did return. The unfavourable weather which detained us so long proved fatal to her, and she was wrecked a few miles to the northward of the river's mouth, and every soul on board perished.

The moment this catastrophe was known every European hastened to the spot, and, with feelings of horror, perceived but too plainly, from the appearance of the wreck and the boat, and by finding also the clothes of the crew, that they had reached the shore in safety, and had afterwards all been murdered; but how, or by whom, it was impossible to discover. The most probable conclusion was that the tribes situated around the European dockyard at Hokianga, having meditated for some time past a great war-like expedition, waited the return of this schooner from Sydney to possess themselves of an additional supply of arms and ammunition, which might enable them to take the field with a certainty of conquest. They had regularly purchased the cargo of this vessel by their labour and their merchandise, and the schooner was merely employed to convey it thither from Sydney, for the use of the natives; unhappily for the poor creatures on board, in running for the mouth of the river, she fell to leeward, and got stranded on the beach, in the very territory of that tribe against whom these preparations were made—the tribe intended to be invaded. Though no formal declaration of war had taken place, the tribes well knew the preparations that were making against them, and the nature of the cargo contained in The

Enterprise; falling into the hands of such fierce and vindictive savages, the fate of the crew may be imagined—all our poor fellows were sacrificed to gratify their feelings of revenge.

Mooetara (the friendly chief of Hokianga) no sooner heard of the fate of the vessel and her crew than he hastened with his party to the spot; it was owing to the investigation which then took place that the conclusion was arrived at that all had been murdered. What remained for Mooetara to do (according to their savage notion of what was right) was to take ample revenge on all the hostile tribes that might fall in his way, whether our poor countrymen met their deaths through accident or treachery. Mooetara instantly commenced the work of destruction; and, having made his vengeance complete, he returned laden with spoil. The promptness with which he acted on this melancholy occasion greatly increased the feelings of security possessed by those Englishmen settled on the banks of the river, as it proved to them that he was both able and willing to protect them, and though the dead could not be restored, yet he had inflicted an awful punishment on their murderers.

CHAPTER LVI

FAREWELL TO NEW ZEALAND

On the 21st a fair wind and smooth sea favoured our departure. Early in the morning the natives who were on board assured us everything would facilitate our passing over the bar with safety, and they prepared to leave the ship. When the moment of separation came, it caused a great deal of emotion on both sides. I must confess I felt much affected when I came to rub noses, shake hands, and say "Farewell" to these kind-hearted people. I saw them go over the ship's side, and reflected that I should never behold them more. There is always something repugnant to our feelings in the idea of separating from any being for ever; and as, in this instance, I felt assured that this was our last time of meeting, it cast a gloom over the pleasure the fair wind and smooth sea would otherwise have afforded me. As we fell down towards the river's mouth, and, indeed, as long as their canoes were to be seen, they kept waving their hands towards us.

Thus terminated my visit to the islands of New Zealand. I had arrived with feelings of fear and disgust, and was merely induced to take up a temporary residence amongst the natives, in hopes of finding something new for my pencil in their peculiar and picturesque style of life. I left them with opinions, in many respects, very favourable towards them. It is true, they are cunning and over-reaching in trade, and filthy in their persons. In regard to the former, we Europeans, I fear, set them a bad example; of the latter, they will gradually amend. Our short visit to Kororarika greatly improved them in that particular. All took great pains to come as clean as possible when they attended our "evening tea-parties." In my opinion, their sprightly, free, and independent deportment, together with their kindness and attention to strangers, compensates for many defects.

On looking round upon their country, an Englishman cannot fail to feel gratified when he beholds the good already resulting to these poor savages from their intercourse with his countrymen; and they themselves are fully sensible of, and truly grateful for, every mark of kindness manifested towards them. They have stores full of the finest Indian corn, which they consider a great luxury, a food which requires little trouble in preparing, keeps well, and is very nutritious. It is but a few years since this useful grain was introduced amongst them; and I sincerely hope this introduction may be followed up, not only by our sending out to them seeds of vegetables and fruits, but by our forwarding to them every variety of quadruped which can be used for food. Abundance of the finest water-melons are daily brought alongside vessels entering their ports; these, in point of flavour, are superior to any I ever met with. I have no doubt every variety of European produce essential to the support of life would thrive equally well; and as food became abundant, and luxuries were introduced, their disgusting feasts on human flesh would soon be discontinued altogether.

We were soon at sea, and speedily felt considerable apprehensions as to the safe termination of our voyage. Our vessel (the brig Governor Macquarie) we well knew was a leaky one, though her leaks did not distress us on the outward voyage, she being then only in ballast trim; but now that she was loaded to the water's edge, and the winter coming on, we became greatly alarmed for her. Another disagreeable circumstance was having no bread or flour on board. To obviate the first evil, and to save the sailors a great deal of hard labour, our Captain offered to give a passage to Sydney to several natives, who accepted his offer, they being always anxious to see the colony; we likewise had on board the great Chief from the Thames, who had caused us so much trouble at Kororarika. These men, being fine, strong, active young fellows, were indefatigable in their exertions at the pumps; and though we had to contend with much heavy weather, and contrary winds, they kept our vessel pretty dry. The want of bread was not so easily remedied; though our Captain treated it lightly, saying he was sure of getting a supply by making a requisition to the missionaries. He accordingly waited upon them, and acquainted them with our distressed condition; they had plenty (for only a few weeks previously they had received a large supply), and as we knew their agent at Sydney, Mr. Campbell, we had no doubt of procuring a sufficiency from them to carry us home; but in this we were disappointed. Captain Kent did not ask them for a supply as a gift, but solicited merely the *loan* of a cask or two till we arrived at Sydney, when he guaranteed that the owners of the brig should return the same quantity into the missionary storehouse there. The little monosyllable *No* was again put in requisition, with this qualification—"that they did not like the Botany Bay skippers." Through their "dislike," the passengers and seamen of the brig might have gone unprovided to sea, had not a "worldly-minded" whaler (fortunately for us) at that critical moment come into port, who, the instant he heard of the ill-success of our entreaty, vented his indignation in pretty coarse language, and said, "if it detained his vessel a week, he would supply us;" and he kept his word; he gave us a bountiful supply, which rendered us comfortable during the whole way home.

It was most interesting to observe our savages when we got well out to sea. They soon appeared to become accustomed to their novel situation, and seemed to feel quite at home and at their ease "on board ship." Their exertions at the pumps were indefatigable. I felt convinced they thought that during all voyages the same labour was gone through to keep the vessel afloat; and as it only required strength and exertion, they cheerfully took that department entirely to themselves, especially as they soon perceived how useless they were when they attempted to perform any other duty on board of the brig, as their knowledge of voyaging extended no further than the distance they go in their own canoes, which, though very beautiful, are sad leaky things at sea; and as, during the time they are out, the greater part of the crew are baling the water out of them, they thought the leaky state of our vessel was no uncommon occurrence. But however cheerfully they worked during the day, nothing could induce them to "turn out" at night; they always stowed themselves away, but in what part of the vessel I never could conjecture. They have a dread of some unknown evil spirit, which they imagine has power over them at night; and this supposition makes them terrible cowards in the dark.

The second day after we were at sea, I saw a group of savages lying round the binnacle, all intently occupied in observing the phenomenon of the magnetic attraction; they seemed at once to comprehend the purpose to which it was applied, and I listened with eager curiosity to their remarks upon it.

"This," said they, "is the white man's God, who directs them safely to different countries, and then can guide them home again." Out of compliment to us, and respect for its wonderful powers, they seemed much inclined to worship this silent little monitor.

During our voyage to Port Jackson we experienced a succession of southerly gales, which Captain Kent informed me were very prevalent at this season of the year. Notwithstanding all our exertions to prevent it, we were carried considerably to leeward of the port. We made Lord Howe's Islands, whose high and bold features rise, as it were, out of the ocean; as we passed close to them, we perceived they were well wooded and watered; and one of the men, who had been on shore there, informed me that there was a tolerably good harbour for small craft. A few miles to the southward of these islands is Ball's Pyramid, a most singular and sublime-looking rock, rising perpendicularly out of the sea to a height of a thousand feet; the base of it is enveloped in perpetual surf, dashing and climbing up its craggy sides. Its appearance, as we saw it, relieved by the setting sun, and the coming on of a stormy night, was awful in the extreme!

Nothing could exceed the delight manifested by our New Zealanders as we sailed up Port Jackson harbour; but, above all, the windmills most astonished them. After dancing and screaming with joy at beholding them, they came running and asking me "if they were not gods." I found they were inclined to attach that sacred appellation to most things they could not understand; they did so when they first became possessed of their muskets, and actually worshipped them, until they discovered how soon they got out of repair, and then, notwithstanding all the prayers they could bestow upon them, they would not mend again of their own accord.

Our Chief from the Thames, who had a great idea of his own dignity, commenced adorning his person, as he felt convinced the Governor would instantly grant him an audience when he came on shore. All our lamps were emptied to add a more beautiful gloss to his hair and complexion; his whole stock of feathers and bones were arranged to the greatest advantage. He at length became quite enraged when he found that he was allowed to sit two days on our deck, amongst all manner of dirty porters and sailors, without either being visited or sent for; and he was loud in his reproaches to us for having deceived him. We certainly were to blame in having induced him to believe we had any influence with the Governor, for however politic we (who had lived in New Zealand) might think it, to pay some attentions to these simple savages, his Excellency, unfortunately, thought otherwise; and though the Chief, attended by his followers, used to sit in the verandah at Government House from morning till night, the Governor never once deigned to speak to them, and they were, in consequence, constantly coming to me with complaints. At length they told me that unless they obtained an audience from our Chief they should consider it so great an insult that they would revenge it upon all the Europeans they could get into their power; and I, well knowing that several families were settled in that part of the country wherein this man was Chief, thought it my duty to let the Governor know, that, however he might dislike their manners and appearance, it might lead to some serious calamity, if he continued to refuse to give them an audience.

I accordingly waited upon the Brigade Major, and explained to him how unwise it was to treat these men with such undisguised contempt. The result was, the Governor saw the affair in the same point of view as myself, and condescended to meet them and converse with them for about five minutes; and with that they were satisfied. Other heads of departments (civil and military) behaved differently, and evidently felt a pleasure in having them with them. The Commander of the troops suffered them to sit at the same table with himself and officers, and had the war-dance performed in the mess-room, which I thought would have brought the house down upon our heads. He likewise permitted them to fall into the ranks with the soldiers, which pleased them beyond everything, inasmuch as they considered it a higher honour in being permitted to stand by our warriors on the martial parade than to take food with our Chiefs at their own table!

The Attorney-General of the colony took a particular interest in these savages, and gave a large party, to which they were invited. Several of the visitors on this occasion came out of curiosity to see how these cannibals would conduct themselves, expecting, no doubt, to witness a display of disgusting gluttony; but in that they were disappointed, for never did any set of men behave with greater decorum than they did.

On being apprised of this invitation, they were all most anxious to obtain European dresses, and when we refused to lend them ours, they requested of our servants the loan of a suit. This being denied them also, with the little money they had they attempted to bargain for whole suits of *convict* dresses, in order to make their *debut* in style at the table of the Attorney-General! When I discovered this to be the case, I explained to them the impropriety of their conduct, and roused their pride by pointing out to them the absurdity of men of their high rank in their own country wishing to appear in the cast-off dress of degraded slaves, and how much more suitable it was to the dignity of their character to appear in their own national costume. Accordingly, on the appointed day, they met the company superbly attired in mats and feathers; they made a splendid show at the dinner-table, and afforded great amusement to the evening visitors. At an early hour they got very sleepy, but were too polite to hint how much they felt oppressed by drowsiness. I saw their eyes grow heavy, and perceived that it was difficult for them to sit upright on their chairs. I mentioned these symptoms to their kind host, who immediately consented to their retiring. They accordingly withdrew into a corner of one of the adjoining rooms, where, lying down huddled together, and covering themselves with their mats, they were soon asleep, and gave no interruption to anyone during the remainder of the evening.

The greatest treat it was in our power to bestow on them was to take them to a review of the troops then stationed at Sydney. The splendour of their regimentals, the regularity of their movements, and the precision of their firing, made them nearly mad with delight; they ran about the plain literally wild with joy, occasionally stopping to gaze with wonder on men performing what they deemed such prodigies. In their ecstasies they occasionally vociferated their own furious war-whoop. Their extravagant expressions of delight, and their many extraordinary gestures, caused great amusement both to the military and to the spectators assembled on the ground; and when the review was over my savage friends were quite exhausted with fatigue and excitement.

After two months' residence at Sydney we had an opportunity of procuring a passage for them to their own country; and they departed, expressing the greatest gratitude for our attentions towards them. They were loaded with presents of all descriptions; for, finding they generally got what they begged for, while here, they importuned everyone they met, and they used daily to return home burthened with the most miscellaneous and extraordinary jumble of commodities it was possible to conceive; for, as everything they then beheld was new to them, and might be (they thought) of some service to them in their own country, each trifle was of great value in their estimation, and was carefully stowed away. They always expressed their concern that so few muskets were given to them, and that they were presented with ammunition in such small quantities. War-like stores were their grand desideratum; and though they would accept of any thing you chose to give them, yet they always had hopes they should finally receive their favourite presents of a stocking of powder, a piece of lead, or a musket.

THE END

APPENDIX

MASSACRE OF CAPT. FURNEAUX'S BOAT'S CREW

CANNIBALISM OF THE MAORIS

[The following is the account given by Captain Furneaux of the massacre of his boat's crew, referred to in Earle's narrative .]

The Resolution, under command of Captain Cook, and the Adventure, commanded by Captain Furneaux, sailed from Plymouth on the 13th April, 1772, to continue the exploration of New Zealand begun during Captain Cook's first voyage. The vessels became finally separated in a gale off Cape Palliser in October, 1773, and the two navigators did not meet again until after Cook's return to England in July, 1775.

Captain Furneaux reported that while his ship was refitting in Queen Charlotte Sound the astronomer's tent was robbed by a party of natives. One who was seen escaping was fired upon and wounded, when he and his confederates made for the woods, leaving their canoe with most of the stolen goods on the shore. "This petty larceny," Captain Furneaux remarks, "probably laid the foundation of that dreadful catastrophe which soon after happened," and which he thus describes:

"On Friday, the 17th, we sent out our large cutter, manned with seven seamen, under the command of Mr. John Rowe, the first mate, accompanied by Mr. Woodhouse, midshipman, and James Tobias Swilley, the carpenter's servant. They were to proceed up the Sound to Grass Cove to gather greens and celery for the ship's company, with orders to return that evening; for the tents had been struck at two in the afternoon, and the ship made ready for sailing the next day. Night coming on, and no cutter appearing, the captain and others began to express great uneasiness. They sat up all night in expectation of their arrival, but to no purpose. At daybreak, therefore, the captain ordered the launch to be hoisted out. She was double manned, and under the command of our second lieutenant, Mr. Burney, accompanied by Mr. Freeman, master, the corporal of marines, with five private men, all well armed, and having plenty of ammunition and three days' provision. They were ordered first to look into East Bay, then to proceed to Grass Cove, and if nothing was to be seen or heard of the cutter there, they were to go farther up the cove, and return by the west shore. Mr. Rowe having left the ship an hour before the time proposed for his departure, we thought his curiosity might have carried him into East Bay, none of our people having ever been there, or that some accident might have happened to the boat, for not the least suspicion was entertained of the natives. Mr. Burney returned about eleven o'clock the same night, and gave us a pointed description of a most horrible scene, described in the following relation:—

"'On Saturday, the 18th, we left the ship about nine o'clock in the morning. We soon got round Long Island and Long Point. We continued sailing and rowing for East Bay, keeping close in shore, and examining with our glasses every cove on the larboard side, till near two o'clock in the afternoon, at which time we stopped at a beach on our left going up East Bay, to dress our dinner.

"'About five o'clock in the afternoon, and within an hour after we had left this place, we opened a small bay adjoining to Grass Cove, and here we saw a large double canoe just hauled upon the beach, with two men and a dog. The two men, on seeing us approach, instantly fled, which made us suspect it was here we should have some tidings of the cutter. On landing and examining the canoe, the first thing we saw therein was one of our cutter's rowlock ports and some shoes, one of which among the latter was known to belong to Mr. Woodhouse. A piece of flesh was found by one of our people, which at first was thought to be some of the salt meat belonging to the cutter's men, but, upon examination, we supposed to be dog's flesh. A most horrid and undeniable proof soon cleared up our doubts, and convinced us we were among no other than cannibals; for, advancing further on the beach, we saw about twenty baskets tied up, and a dog eating a piece of broiled flesh, which, upon examination, we suspected to be human. We cut open the baskets, some of which were full of roasted flesh, and others of fern root, which serves them for bread. Searching others, we found more shoes and a hand, which was immediately known to have belonged to Thos. Hill, one of our forecastle men, it having been tattooed with the initials of his name. We now proceeded a little way in the woods, but saw nothing else. Our next design was to launch the canoe, intending to destroy her; but seeing a great smoke ascending over the nearest hill, we made all possible haste to be with them before sunset.

"'At half after six we opened Grass Cove, where we saw one single and three double canoes, and a great many natives assembled on the beach, who retreated to a small hill, within a ship's length of the water side, where they stood talking to us. On the top of the high land, beyond the woods, was a large fire, from whence, all the way down the hill, the place was thronged like a fair. When we entered the cove, a musketoon was fired at one of the canoes, as we imagined they might be full of men lying down, for they were all afloat, but no one was seen in them. Being doubtful whether their retreat proceeded from fear or a desire to decoy us into an ambuscade, we were determined not to be surprised, and therefore, running close in shore, we dropped the grappling near enough to reach them with our guns, but at too great a distance to be under any apprehensions from their treachery. The savages on the little hill kept their ground, hallooing, and making signs for us to land. At these we now took aim, resolving to kill as many of them as our bullets would reach, yet it was some time before we could dislodge them. The first volley did not seem to affect them much, but on the second they began to scramble away as fast as they could, some howling and others limping. We continued to fire as long as we could see the least glimpse of any of them through the bushes. Among these were two very robust men, who maintained their ground without moving an inch till they found themselves forsaken by all their companions, and then, disdaining to run, they marched off with great composure and deliberation. One of them, however, got a fall, and either lay there or crawled away on his hands and feet; but the other escaped without any apparent hurt. Mr. Burney now improved their panic, and, supported by the marines, leaped on shore and pursued the fugitives. We had not advanced far from the water-side, on the beach, before we met with two bunches of celery, which had been gathered by the cutter's crew. A broken oar was stuck upright in the ground, to which the natives had tied their canoes, whereby we were convinced this was the spot where the attack had been made. We now searched all along at the back of the beach, to see if the cutter was there, but instead of her, the most horrible scene was presented to our view; for there lay the hearts, heads, and lungs of several of our people, with hands and limbs in a mangled condition, some broiled and some raw; but no other parts of their bodies, which made us suspect that the cannibals had feasted upon and devoured the rest. At a little distance we saw the dogs gnawing their entrails. We observed a large body of the natives collected together on a hill about two miles off, but as night drew on apace, we could not advance to such a distance; neither did we think it safe to attack them, or even to quit the shore to take an account of the number killed, our troop being a very small one, and the savages were both numerous, fierce, and much irritated. While we remained almost stupefied on the spot, Mr. Fannen said that he heard the cannibals assembling in the woods, on which we returned to our boat, and having hauled alongside the canoes, we demolished three of them. During this transaction the fire on the top of the hill disappeared, and we could hear the savages in the woods at high words, quarrelling, perhaps, on account of their different opinions, whether they should attack us and try to save their canoes. They were armed with long lances, and weapons not unlike a sergeant's halbert in shape, made of hard wood, and mounted with bone instead of iron. We suspected that the dead bodies of our people had been divided among those different parties of cannibals who had been concerned in the massacre, and it was not improbable that the group we saw at a distance by the fire were feasting upon some of them, as those on shore had been where the remains were found, before they had been disturbed by our unexpected visit. Be that as it may, we could discover no traces of more than four of our friends' bodies, nor could we find the place where the cutter was concealed. It now grew dark, on which account we collected carefully the remains of our mangled friends, and, putting off, made the best of our way from this polluted place. When we opened the upper part of the Sound, we saw a very large fire about three or four miles higher up, which formed a complete oval, reaching from the top of a hill down almost to the water-side, the middle space being enclosed all round by the fire, like a hedge. Mr. Burney and Mr. Fannen having consulted together, they were both of opinion that we could, by an attempt, reap no other advantage than the poor satisfaction of killing some more of the savages. Upon leaving Grass Cove we had fired a volley towards where we heard the Indians talking, but by going in and out of the boat our pieces had got wet, and four of them missed fire. What rendered our situation more critical, it began to rain, and our ammunition was more than half expended. We, for these reasons, without spending time where nothing could be hoped for but revenge, proceeded for the ship, and arrived safe aboard before midnight.'"

It is a little remarkable that Captain Furneaux had been several times up Grass Cove with Captain Cook, where they saw no inhabitants, and no other signs of any but a few deserted villages, which appeared as if they had not been occupied for many years, and yet, in Mr. Burney's opinion, when he entered the same cove, there could not be less than fifteen hundred or two thousand people.

On Thursday, the 23rd of December, the Adventure departed from, and made sail out of, the Sound. She stood to the eastward, to clear the straits, which was happily effected the same evening; but the ship was baffled for two or three days with light winds before she could clear the coast. In this interval of time the chests and effects of the ten men who had been murdered were sold before the mast, according to an old sea custom.

When Captain Cook was in the Sound on his third voyage, he learned that the massacre arose over an unpremeditated quarrel. Kahura, who had been active in the tragedy, told Cook that a Maori having brought a stone hatchet to barter, the man to whom it was offered took it, and would neither return it nor give anything for it, and on which the owner snatched some bread from the party of Europeans, who were at dinner on the beach, as an equivalent, and then the quarrel began. Kahura himself had a narrow escape of being shot, while another was shot beside him; and the Europeans, outnumbered, were surrounded and killed. It was also stated by the natives that not one of the shots fired by the party of Captain Furneaux led by Mr. Burney to search for the missing people had taken effect so as to kill or even to hurt a single person.

APPENDIX

THE DEATH OF WHAREUMU (KING GEORGE)

The death of this Bay of Islands chief, who acted as protector to Mr. Earle during his residence at Kororareka, is thus described by Messrs. Hobbs and Stack, Wesleyan missionaries at Hokianga, in a letter dated from Mangungu, Hokianga, on the 22nd March, 1828:—

"On the same day that Hongi died at Whangaroa a son of the late Pomare's, named Tiki, was killed at Waima by a chief of the tribe called Mahurihuri. Waima is in Hokianga, and only a few miles distance from us. The cause of the quarrel was this: Tiki had had some of his pigs stolen by the natives of Waima, and he was seeking utu by robbing their sweet potato plantations, for which he was shot.

"As soon as the report of the young man's death reached the Bay of Islands, 400 natives collected together, forming two divisions, under two separate chiefs, Whareumu, or, as he is called by the Europeans, King George, and Toi, and came to Hokianga. Toi and his party arrived first at Waima, where he found Patuone and all the natives and other chiefs of our district. After robbing the natives of Waima of their potatoes, etc., peace was made, and no further evil consequences seemed likely to arise. The next day, the 14th, Whareumu and his party arrived. He was highly displeased with Toi for having made peace on such easy terms. He prevailed upon him, therefore, to break his league. Whareumu was also very insolent to Muriwai, intimated that he was a coward, and poured contempt upon the idea of the Hokianga natives standing in their own defence. On the morning of the 15th a quarrel ensued between the 400 Bay of Islanders and the natives of Waima, our natives also having now become their allies. This fray did not at the outset seem likely to be attended with fatal results, but, as Solomon justly observes, the beginning of strife is like the letting out of water; so it was in this instance. Shots were fired on both sides till several were killed and wounded. At length Muriwai, who was a pacificator, was wounded and fell. Supposing he was killed, our natives (for the natives of

Waima fled as soon as matters assumed a serious aspect) no longer regarded matters lightly, but turned round in great rage, for they also were in the act of retreating, and singled out Whareumu as a satisfaction for Muriwai. Whareumu received two balls before he was killed. The one which killed him went through his throat. As soon as he fell all his followers fled, leaving about nine of their companions dead on the field, amongst whom was Oro, the chief who commenced our Whangaroa robbing. This ended the contest. Patuone and Nene immediately took up the body of the fallen chief and made great lamentation over him, and have since placed his body between the bodies of their own relations as a mark of respect."

Lightning Source UK Ltd.
Milton Keynes UK
UKOW052021230212

187816UK00001B/156/A